# NORTH CHESHIRE

Edited by Lucy Jeacock

First published in Great Britain in 2002 by
*YOUNG WRITERS*
Remus House,
Coltsfoot Drive,
Peterborough, PE2 9JX
Telephone  (01733) 890066

HB ISBN 0 75433 774 X
SB ISBN 0 75433 775 8

# FOREWORD

This year, the Young Writers' Hidden Treasures competition proudly presents a showcase of the best poetic talent from over 72,000 up-and-coming writers nationwide.

Young Writers was established in 1991 and we are still successful, even in today's technologically-led world, in promoting and encouraging the reading and writing of poetry.

The thought, effort, imagination and hard work put into each poem impressed us all, and once again, the task of selecting poems was a difficult one, but nevertheless, an enjoyable experience.

We hope you are as pleased as we are with the final selection and that you and your family continue to be entertained with *Hidden Treasures North Cheshire* for many years to come.

# CONTENTS

| | |
|---|---|
| James Milton | 52 |
| Sam Hyde | 52 |
| Caitlin Elston | 53 |
| Emma Hollows | 53 |
| Kate Davies | 54 |
| Cara Janes | 54 |
| Andrew Hamilton | 55 |
| Grace Watson | 56 |
| Samantha Walters | 56 |
| Michael English | 57 |
| Aymen Alshawi | 57 |
| Ryan Hession | 58 |
| Helena Wright | 58 |
| Ashley Cleary | 59 |
| Hope Weir | 59 |
| Katie Higgins | 60 |
| Ross Atkinson | 60 |
| Tejal Patel | 61 |
| Henry Naylor | 61 |
| Sam Hughes | 62 |
| Emily Hough | 62 |
| Daniel Fisher | 63 |
| Kerry Anne | 63 |
| Ben Winby | 64 |
| Gareth Williams | 64 |
| Laura Heywood | 65 |
| Rorie Sparkes | 66 |
| Gabriella Farrell | 67 |
| Chudi Emeagi | 68 |
| Tim Wormald | 68 |
| Jack Smallshaw | 69 |
| Daniel King | 69 |
| Gavin Dixon | 70 |
| Charlotte Brownlee | 71 |
| Oliver Janes | 72 |
| Genevieve Riley | 73 |
| Claire English | 74 |

| | |
|---|---|
| Nick Thomson | 75 |
| Vicky Fleming | 76 |
| Stephanie Hough | 77 |
| Rishabh Agrawal | 78 |
| Dominic Cole | 78 |
| Lucy Wood | 79 |
| Emma Doyle | 80 |
| James Hamilton | 81 |
| Euan Mackway-Jones | 82 |
| James Smith | 82 |
| Hayley White | 83 |
| Hannah Sanders | 84 |
| Joseph O'Driscoll | 84 |
| Lewis Clarke | 85 |
| Melissa Bates | 85 |
| David Robert Peckitt | 86 |
| Stephen Johnson | 87 |
| George Gallagher | 87 |
| Jenny Hamilton | 88 |
| Peter Screeton | 88 |
| Richard Schenk | 89 |
| Clare Bennett | 90 |
| Philip Jackman | 91 |
| James Lewis | 92 |
| Olivia Grant-Caren | 92 |
| Charlotte Richards | 93 |
| Zoe Griffiths | 93 |
| Tim Blower | 94 |

## Castle View Primary School

| | |
|---|---|
| Adam Cosgrove | 94 |
| Toni-Lea Deane | 95 |
| Jodie Carroll | 95 |
| Hayley Holden | 96 |
| Christopher Joyce | 96 |
| Emma-Lee Butterworth | 97 |

| | |
|---|---|
| Laura Voss | 149 |
| Robert Grainger | 149 |
| Amanda Orme | 150 |
| Chelsea Morgan | 150 |
| Nathan Southern | 151 |
| Charlotte McCormick | 151 |
| Nikki Williams | 151 |
| Chelsea Davies | 152 |
| Amy Brown | 152 |
| Wade Johnston | 152 |
| Joel Yates | 153 |
| Sophie Spencer-Duggan | 153 |
| Kate Healey | 153 |
| Kerry Horabin | 154 |
| Anthony Moore | 154 |
| Elisha Storrow | 154 |
| Andrew Kelley | 155 |
| Zoe Pullan | 155 |
| Natalie Lloyd | 156 |
| Laura Bentley | 156 |

St Mary's CE Primary School, Sale

| | |
|---|---|
| Rebecca Perkins | 157 |
| Ella Billson | 157 |
| Sarah Donovan | 158 |
| Siân Whitefoot | 158 |
| Sally Jowett | 159 |
| Katherine Deverell-Smith | 159 |
| Lucy Longmore | 160 |
| Robert Hardwick | 160 |
| Emily Mann | 161 |
| Helen Robinson | 161 |
| Harry Raphael | 162 |
| Thomas Biddulph | 162 |
| Charlotte Edmondson | 163 |
| Adam Martell | 163 |

## St Vincent's RC Primary School, Knutsford

| | |
|---|---|
| Frankie Brown | 164 |
| Cathal McGoohan | 164 |
| Luke Fletcher | 165 |
| Abigail Stones | 165 |
| Gemma Whyatt | 166 |
| Eleanor Regan | 166 |
| David McCulloch | 167 |
| Caitlin Julia Rowlands | 168 |
| Ishbel Johnson | 168 |
| George Morris | 169 |
| Charlotte Perls | 169 |
| Francesca Spada | 170 |
| Jessica Whyatt | 170 |
| Amy Yardley | 171 |
| Amy Haughey | 171 |
| Mica McDonald | 172 |
| Epiphany Harrop | 172 |
| Christopher Clarke | 173 |
| Francesca Whyatt | 173 |
| David McCabe | 174 |
| Camilla Nixon | 174 |
| Nathan Dodd | 175 |
| Marco Granata | 175 |
| Thomas Fletcher | 176 |
| Emma Hobson | 176 |
| Charles Miller | 177 |
| Cameron Mair | 178 |
| Amy Morgan | 178 |
| Georgia Jackson | 179 |
| Stephanie Trafford | 179 |
| Rupert Heap | 180 |
| Rosie Long | 180 |
| Hannah Paver | 181 |

## St Wilfrid's RC Primary School, Northwich

| | |
|---|---|
| Emma Phillips | 181 |
| Rebecca Cutbill | 182 |

| | |
|---|---|
| Kate Frazer | 182 |
| Anna Cartwright | 183 |
| James Turrell | 184 |
| Jemima Hollingworth | 184 |
| Emma Draffin | 185 |
| Jennifer Schofield | 186 |
| Rebecca Boyle | 187 |
| Genevieve Reynolds | 188 |
| Felicity Lewis | 188 |
| Brian Byrne | 189 |
| Isabel Murray | 189 |
| Emma Hitch | 190 |
| Michael Thomas | 190 |
| David Rattigan | 191 |
| Amy Fallon | 192 |
| Leah Whyment | 192 |
| Jane Edwards | 193 |
| Michael Jones | 193 |
| Colleen O'Sullivan | 194 |
| Dean McGuinness | 194 |
| Richard Tranter | 195 |
| Michelle Huggon | 195 |
| Avril Wood | 196 |
| Alex Plant | 196 |
| Ben Millar | 197 |
| Shanice Ashley | 198 |
| Geneviève Darwin | 198 |
| Claire Campbell | 199 |
| Catherine Lewis | 199 |
| Cameron Mackay | 200 |
| John Peyton | 200 |
| Christopher Timm | 201 |

Sandiway County Primary School

| | |
|---|---|
| Richard Roper | 201 |
| James Pearson | 202 |
| Douglas Pinnington | 203 |
| Alexander Crompton | 204 |

# The Poems

# PEACE AND WAR

Peace is paradise, quiet and calm,
War is like a noisy alarm.
Peace is like people on park benches,
War is soldiers in dirty trenches.
Peace is a graceful swan,
War is time-wasting long!

War is terrifying,
Mean and nasty.
Killing people so they're in pain,
Eating up buildings
With balls of hot fire to destroy!

War is a pack of blood-sucking hounds,
Peace is people worrying in crowds.
War is a sizzling monster waiting to leap,
Peace is people running on their feet!

Peace is soft and sweet like sticky toffee pudding,
It's harmless unlike a volcano burning up.
Just calm, nice
And completely under control!

Which one would you choose?
War and lose
Or just peace
Harmless and quiet?

*Reagen Cooper  (10)*
*Brooklands CP School*

1

## PLAYING IN THE PADDLING POOL IN SUMMER

*Chorus:*
Splash, splash, splish, splash,
Playing in a pool of water,
Splash, splash, splish, splash,
Playing in the water.

Butterflies flying in all directions,
Birds tweeting a happy tune,
The summer sun is warming me,
So I'll be burnt quite soon!

*Chorus*

Flowers swaying here and there,
Grass growing everywhere!
Bees buzzing in my ear,
I am swimming when I stare!

*Chorus*

**Katie Jeffree  (9)**
**Brooklands CP School**


## SUMMER

Here we are right in the summer,
Looking like it's hot outside,
Smell the slight scent of flowers growing,
Looks like we're having lunch outside.

Here we come with the birds singing nicely,
I'll have to wear short summer clothes,
Butterflies flittering through the air,
But here comes the slight breeze.

Running rabbits look like going down rapids,
The shining sun makes the blazing heat,
The brilliant view of the snow-topped mountains,
As the summer scent goes by.

*Sean Farrell  (9)*
*Brooklands CP School*


## RAINY DAY

*Chorus:*
Jumping in puddles is really fun
'Now stop it,' shouted my mum
My rain hat flew off and went down the street
I screamed at my mum, *'I want something to eat.'*
It's bitter cold
I'm starting to mould
It's all grey and cloudy

*Verse 1:*
I saw a puddle so I jumped in it
I forgot I was wearing my new city kit.
'Look what you've done now!' shouted my mum
'You've got mud all over your bum.'

*Chorus*

*Verse 2:*
Look, it's stopped raining
Oh no! It's not, it is gaining
Look, all the slugs are coming out
The air smells fresh, there's no doubt.

*Chorus*

*Emma Lucy Littlefair  (9)*
*Brooklands CP School*

# WAR AND PEACE

War is a horror film
A brutal beast tearing lives apart.
Peace is smooth and gentle
Delightful like a sunny day.
War shatters lives
Spirals of flames like killing machines.
Peace is heavenly harmony
Angels of happiness and joy.

War is destructive
Jagged and dark.
Peace is like pancakes,
Scrumptious and hot.
War is dead people
In a lake of blood.
Peace is happiness
Joy to the world.

War is insane
People dying at war's heels.
Peace is exciting
Friendly with all.
War is a devil
That's escaped from Hell.
Peace is soft,
Cuddly and calm.

War is a gang
Of millions of murderers.
Peace is a nightingale,
A smooth song putting people to sleep.
War is a goblin
Hitting people with bats.
Peace is relaxing
Like an hour-long massage,
Which one would you have?
Gunfire or joy?

*Jacob Weir (11)*
*Brooklands CP School*


## WAR AND PEACE

War is like a death field,
Peace is like a large shield,
Peace is restful, delightful and shy,
So be peaceful and you may be able to fly.

Peace is soft, cool and calm,
And it is all in a person's palm,
War is destructive and cruel,
And all the soldiers want to rule.

Peace will not kill and slay,
War is not willing to pay,
War is a vomiting volcano,
So do not ask for peace because the answer will be no.

War is a dart,
Hitting you in the heart,
Peace will not kill and slay,
So be glad we have peace today.

*Ahmed Alshawi (10)*
*Brooklands CP School*

## WAR AND PEACE

War is a towering tornado,
Raging through the devastation.
As hungry as a bald eagle,
Taking men's lives in the nation.

But peace is as calm as the summer's breeze,
Drifting along like a delicate dove.
As tasty as a sugary cake,
Full of caring and love.

War has power, but it still isn't free,
Using all its strength and all its might.
Never stopping, full of revenge,
Still fighting into the dead of each night.

*Hooray!* Peace is a tranquil harmony of Heaven,
Which will always be the way that is right.
Shy and restful . . . patient and kind,
Much better than having a fight.

War is terrible, raging like the sea,
Like a pack of evil hounds.
But peace is as gentle as a tropical breeze,
With blissful, beautiful sounds.

Gently floating on the clouds,
Peace will always be.
There'll be no more war cos war is locked up,
And peace holds the key.

As quick as war started,
War will end.
But peace is eternal,
And peace still lives on.

War is a desolate death field,
But peace is a precious, perfect, paradise!

*Chukwuma Okpalugo (10)*
*Brooklands CP School*

## WAR AND PEACE

War is a bulldozer tearing up humanity,
War defines the word insanity,
Peace is a soft, white dove taking to flight,
It's a candle glowing in the dead of night.
War is like a death field,
With its own shiny, silver shield.

Peace is loyal, calm and warm,
War is a dream of harmony ripped and torn,
Peace echoes through the land,
War is a poor soldier killed at demand.

War is a bloodthirsty beast,
War is the feeling when it is released.
Peace is a beautiful white horse,
And it runs along its sandy brown course.

Peace is the calm summer breeze,
Peace is anything you can seize.
War is invincible Hell's flames,
War is a bully, calling you names.

*Katy Cleary (10)*
*Brooklands CP School*

## WAR AND PEACE

War is like Satan with amputated legs
Covered with bazookas and nuclear bombs
Cloaking the world in layer of black thickness
Peace is a baby wearing a halo
As tranquil and as innocent as the blue tropical sea
The safest path to Heaven . . . that is what peace is

The flames of Hell lick the Afghans
Tempting the people to a world of gory deaths
With its transparent black bribes
Peace is shy, distraught, cautious,
'How can I live?' it asks itself
'In this suffocated, choking world?'

War is an army tank bulldozing all of humanity
But what are the consequences?
People meeting the Cybruses
Rowing down the dark waters of death
And knocking on the doors of Hades

Peace is judicious
Peace is a paradise
Not known to many
Where the turtle doves fly,
With olive branches in their beaks

War is as bitter as gall
As sombre as a judge
Crunch! Crunch!
Tearing up families
Tearing up the lives of brave soldiers
That is what the savage beast does

War is the past, present and future,
Of this ungoverned world
The next generation will bring plasma cannons and more

Unless peace can infiltrate
This world of slavery
Which one will you choose?
A dustbin of corpses
Or a life of harmony forever long?

*Rahul Chattopadhyay (10)*
*Brooklands CP School*


## WAR AND PEACE

War is fearful, brutal evil,
Peace is full of loving generous people.
War is full of clumsy, threatening humans
Peace is crowded with friendly men and women.
War is frightening all humanity,
Peace is flowing through houses with happiness.

War is speeding through the lands,
Peace glows in people's hands.
War is controlled by all the demons,
Peace is made by the kindest people.
War takes over humans' property,
Peace is treated with no harm.

War can last years and years,
Peace will last as long as everyone cheers.
War will destroy mankind forever,
Peace will take care of violence and ungratefulness.
War will kill lots of people,
Peace will keep us together for as long as we shall live.

Peace is one choice,
War another.
Which one will you choose,
Apart or together?

*Matthew Shaw (10)*
*Brooklands CP School*

## WAR AND PEACE

Peace is reading on a bench,
War is crashing as loud as trenches.
Peace is a walk on the beach on a summer's day,
War is a booming, boring play.
Peace is doing things all day,
War is the slashing noise from swords and knives.

Peace is a soft, tropical ocean,
War is death and blood.
Peace is a restful, delightful, bright blue sky,
War is killing and horrible.
Peace is enjoyment at the weekend,
War is nasty and sick.

Peace is beautiful birds flying,
While friendly brave soldiers are dying.
Peace is drinking Carling,
War is people parling.
Peace is nice and kind,
War is people getting fined.

You remember this poem,
It's telling a lesson.
You can choose but the best for you
But with peace you can do what you want.

*Ben Ainsworth  (10)*
*Brooklands CP School*


## ON A FROSTY, COLD, WINTER'S MORNING

It's very kind of windy
Foggy in the air.
Ice is on the ponds
And children are playing out in the frosty, cold evening.
When the evening comes the snow starts falling down
And all the trees are covered in very thick snow

And you must have your coats, gloves and hats!
Cars are not driving because of the snow.
Snowmen are dancing up and down the roads
And everywhere is snowy
And I want to play but I can't.

*Ria Lessiter  (8)*
*Brooklands CP School*


## WAR AND PEACE

War is terror, screams and guns
Making people fall into death traps
Peace is great, smooth and gentle
Kind, friendly with everyone

War is brave soldiers dying
Battlefields of half bodies
Peace is a great white dove in the air
Making friendship everywhere

War is like Hell and hatred
Chopping people to their knees
Peace is like Heaven playing
With their clouds and halo

War is amputated legs
With injuries, even the death of millions
Peace is harmony, tranquillity and love
All put together

War is terror, cries and scream
Peace is gentle with gleams
So respect the one that you know is right
And be thankful for those who lost their lives
To save our own souls.

*Chris Pugh  (10)*
*Brooklands CP School*

# WAR AND PEACE

War is a brutal bloodshed,
Like a tornado, killing all,
Peace is a calm, blue sea,
Like walking on fluffy, white clouds,
War is the pits of Hell,
Satan enjoyed to hear the screams,
Of innocents that fell.

Peace is a gentle breeze,
For the dove that comes gliding down,
*Boom!* Sound the destructive guns,
Fierce, snarling, snapping, the Devil's dogs,
War is taking people's lives,
Peace is a tropical paradise,
Love, happiness and tranquillity.

War is endless streams of unhappy tears,
Of people losing lives,
Of people with constant fears,
Peace is pure and divine,
A gentle feather floating from the sky.

War is sinister clouds in the sky,
A journey over hot coals,
A devastating, destructive notion,
People die for their country,
But war is never won.

Peace is almost Heaven,
Precious and serene,
A bunch of beautiful flowers,
Lying on a sunkissed beach,
Pure bliss, undisturbed.

Peace is freedom,
But war could be stopped . . .

*Sam Moorhouse  (10)*
*Brooklands CP School*


## WAR AND PEACE

War breaks out and the warning alarm starts
To sound its siren for the people to hear,
Everyone starts racing around
To get into a shelter that's near,
Peace will be in the countryside
Where all evacuees go during the war,
All the children have been evacuated for sure,
Throughout the duration of the war.

Peace is a breezy, sunny day in the summer,
Where children happily play,
War is a gigantic hurricane
Which whirls and whooshes anything and everything in its path
Through night and day.

War is a time where families get separated
And cry until the end of their days,
Peace is a never-ending road to joy
As everyone says.

*Antonia Duffin  (10)*
*Brooklands CP School*

# WAR AND PEACE

The war is the death, a killing beast,
It sets loose the hounds of Hell, with killing teeth,
Bombs are falling, just like soldiers,
Everyone killed by the murderous monsters,
Then Satan appears, in all his glory,
Anything in war is very gory.

Peace is a blessing, a white dove sails,
Singing its song and all hate fails,
No more fighting, darkness is lightening,
Peace is shy, doesn't appear often,
But when it does, everything will soften.

War is an omen, the worst of them all,
The omen of death makes everyone fall,
It is a killer,
An absolute chiller,
To children a thriller,
And all caused by Hitler.

Peace too is an omen, the omen of kindness,
Any field you walk upon, is utterly mineless.
The volcano of anger, erupts no longer,
All is fine, there is no pain, hopefully there won't be war again,
All is sweet, peace is fantastic, hopefully there won't be war again.

The savage beast with shrieks from Hell,
With a crunch, crunch, another man fell,
Never to tell, his story again.
War kills, it is dangerous and bad, let us hope peace can rule.
War is murdersome, a killer and bad, let us hope peace can rule.

*Daniel Corker  (10)*
*Brooklands CP School*

## BONFIRE NIGHT

The frosty air surrounds us all,
While we wait for the bonfire and the fireworks,
We're all dressed up in our fleeces and coats,
Little voices are playing with splendid sparklers,
Look there's the man with the match come to light the bonfire,
I feel like a cat with a new ball of wool,
Suddenly the fire is alight.

There's a big, fiery, frightful dragon pelting out fire at me,
The beast is jumping and bumping,
As bright as the moonlight sky,
It twirls and swirls like a plane in the air,
The fiery dragon yaps and barks up into the night.

5, 4, 3, 2, 1, whoo . . . bang, crash, whizz,
The 'soaring star' glides into the sky,
Swirling, whirling, a sudden spark of light fills up the ebony black sky,
The 'Retro jet' as red as a red, red rose,
The Christmas tree, the silver palm,
The Chrysanthemum sparks like a charm,
Rockets soar into the sky showing off the vast, blank night,
Then at last the concluding rocket disappears
Into the big, black hole of the night.

The bonfire withers away, dead and dull,
Woolly jumpers, woven hats,
Folk walk home to the warmth of their house,
So again, up above, the empty, big, black sky,
As silent as a mystical wood,
But what do I hear, another bang over there,
*Goodbye, see you again another year!*

***Holly Holder (11)***
***Brooklands CP School***

# WAR AND PEACE!

War is . . .

War is the pits of Hell,
A journey down to the dark underworld,
Over the burning coal screaming,
Houses disappearing, children leaving,
War is like an evil curse,
Bodies being blown to bits,
Tears being shed by the families left at home to work, work, work,
To die of hunger or loneliness.

Peace is . . .
Peace is like a sweet spring breeze,
An endless, exquisite, enjoyable dream,
A perfect paradise where everyone's free,
Its harmony echoing through the land,
Bringing people together hand by hand,
Peace is heavenly, friendly and shy,
Laughter, singing, not tears or cries,
Its wishes coming true for every person,
Water cascading down a slippery slope.

War is . . .
War is atrocious, appalling and mean,
Let's pray and hope there's no World War Three,
Innocent babies being born to what?
A destroyed world with millions gone,
Crunch . . . Crunch . . . Satan's fangs,
Piercing human hearts destroying human souls,
Humanity coughing constantly,
Under the gas-filled cordite air.

Peace is . . .
Peace is meandering through the clouds,
Birds singing when you wake up in the morning,
Travelling off the Earth into the peaceful cosmic zone,
No one to bother you, you're all alone,
Peace is restful, happy, the best,
A serene swan on a misty lake drifting . . . drifting . . . drifting.
War and peace are . . .

Peace and war are like sugar and salt,
Completely different - opposites,
Bloody battles against families and friends
Good or bad,
Health or disease,
Kind or evil,
Pleasure or pain . . .
*Right or wrong!*

*Stephanie Tait  (11)*
*Brooklands CP School*


## SNOW DAY

As it was a snow day
I got up and put my coat, scarf, gloves, boots and tracksuit on.
As I walked along it was pitch white colour
Well, most of it was.
Ice blocks and dark cloud above.
Whistling wind as the big chill passed
And the snow crunching as I walk
And the fog makes it end.
I sit by the fire.

*Anthony M Bleackley  (8)*
*Brooklands CP School*

## WAR AND PEACE

War is a crafty criminal
Waiting to strike
Peace is a beige butterfly
Fluttering away in the breeze

Bang goes the bomb
Striking a house where a family lay
Peace is chocolate getting eaten away

War is Hell
With its fiery hot ashes
Peace is Heaven
Wearing a halo each day

War is a black beast
With its fearful fangs
Peace is a newly born lamb
All fluffy and white

War is black
Soulless and dark
Peace is white
All the colours of the rainbow

War is a trench
A murderous hole
Trees are peace
Along with the green grass

War is a bloody battle
Hundreds of people dying
Peace is all living things working together
Peace is harmony

Peace will always live on
But war could be stopped forever.

*Christopher Yuille  (11)*
*Brooklands CP School*

## WAR AND PEACE

War is like the pits of Hell,
Brave and bold were the soldiers that fell,
Destroying anything that lies in its way,
War is a dark and gruesome day.

Peace is like a fluttering dove,
The choirs sing from up above,
Meadows of flowers cover the land,
Peace is a paradise with its golden sand.

War is a beast hunting for prey,
Peace is the sun shimmering each day,
War is as sour as lemon and lime,
Peace is as sweet as all things divine.

Peace is restful, delightful and shy,
Flying through the clouds up in the sky,
Freedom and joy to the world,
Peace is Heaven in a tropical whirl.

War is like a pool of blood,
Fighting back as hard as they could,
Gripping their triggers with their hands,
Out of the guns came some gigantic,
*Bangs* . . .

Silence came to the world,
No more war . .. only peace,

Peace is Heaven . . .
War is Hell . . .

*Helen Tait (11)*
*Brooklands CP School*

## WAR AND PEACE

War is like death
With his sickly scythe.
Peace is a serene sea
Trickling up the golden brown beach.

Bullets dig through soldiers' bodies
Knocking them down, never again to rise.
Tin cans crush soldiers
Like they're blind;
Then rumbling over a tank trap
Ejecting their dead crew.
*Bang! Crash!*

Peace is a place
With no fighting and killing.
A bird spreads harmony
As it flies over the land.
In peace you can walk through cloud,
Surrounded by glittering powder.
*Swish!*

*Ian Brocklebank  (11)*
*Brooklands CP School*


## EVENING

Evening comes
When the moon is shining
Evening comes
When I am crying
Evening comes
When you are reading
Evening comes
When I am eating

Evening comes
When you are watching
Evening comes
When I am singing
Evening comes
When owls are hooting
Evening comes
When I am sleeping.

*Olivia Richards  (8)*
*Brooklands CP School*

## WAR AND PEACE

War is a mad exploding volcano
Peace is a peaceful sunshine city
With pretty petals where sun rays shine.
War is a filthy puddle of mud
With rapid revolvers and muddy trenches.

Peace is a beautiful walk on a long summer's day,
War is a destructive killing machine with bloody trenches.

Peace is a lovely beam from Heaven
Shining down on you.
War is full of Hell's flames
Trying to make you bleed.

Peace is a silver shield
Free from the battlefield in Hell.
War is a brutal beast
With bombs covering up the sky.

*Oliver Bowden  (11)*
*Brooklands CP School*

# PEACE AND WAR

War is like the pits of Hell
Where dark clouds twist and turn
Peace is a sweet, sugary smell
Filling a tranquil harmony of Heaven

War is a towering tornado
Sweeping midnight skies
That is why I hate it
Many people die

Peace is a fluttering, flying dove
Shimmering in the sun
Peace is a wonderful place for love
With puffs of glistening powder all around

Peace is like being on a deserted island
Or in a world of heaven
War is a pack of evil hounds
That turn the sky to blood

All we want is peace!
Is that too much to ask?

*Katie Coe  (10)*
*Brooklands CP School*

# SUMMERTIME

One fine summer's morning
As I get up
I can hear birds
Singing summer songs.

As I walk outside
After breakfast
I can smell the summer fragrance from flowers.

As I walk to the park
I can taste summer fruits
And I can see busy bees collecting nectar.

As I walk home
I can see the sun smile
As it says 'Goodnight.'

*Aamna Khan (8)*
*Brooklands CP School*

## WAR AND PEACE

War is destruction, death, a destroyer,
Peace is beautiful, caring, a sweet butterfly.
War's heart does not care about life,
Forever laughing at those who suffer.
Peace is calm, sharing with its friends
And loving everything.

War is an erupting, screaming volcano,
Burning all in its way.
Peace is a soft, shining flower petal
Gleaming in the joyous day.
War is horrible, mean and cruel
But peace is graceful, kind and sweet.

So remember this poem,
You've got to be sure,
Should you pick peace,
Or should you pick war?

*Arran Johnson (11)*
*Brooklands CP School*

# WAR AND PEACE!

War is as painful for soldiers as burning in Hell,
But even more painful for families.
They are torn apart,
With a single letter as their only communication.
War is the Devil,
Laughing at every death that takes place between two countries,
But injures and kills both sides of the battle.
War is a dirty, detestable, death-causing devil!
And has not a bit of good in it!

Peace is a tranquil paradise adored by all,
It is the lord of the angels,
Playing a sweet song on his golden harp down to us from the heavens.
Peace is the way that the Lord wanted us to live.
Peace is the dove,
Flying freely with such grace.
Peace is the sound of a trickling stream,
And children playing in an open field.
Peace is the most tranquil thing on Earth,
As joyful as a baby's birth.
It is the sound of a Sekaddas singing,
High up in the trees,
Flying, flying, flying freely.

War is a beast,
Ripping out every form of life,
Destroying dreams,
Ruining lives.
War is a cannon barrel,
Leaving behind a field of bloody bodies,
Only to break the hearts of wives and children.
War is thousands of children being evacuated,
War is many families being separated.

Peace is a heaven of harmony filled with joy and laughter,
A calm, happy place where every form of life can be cheerful
and cheery.
Peace could not be more the opposite of war,
It is filled with love and friendship,
Whereas war is filled with loathing and hate.
Peace is the summer sun,
And a soft, warm breeze
Peace is a paradise so great,
That everyone loves.
No one could ever want war,
For war is not won,
It only destroys lives instead.
Peace is the way that we should live,
And we should be glad that we have peace today,
Though we still want to make peace throughout the world one day.

*Megan McCrudden (10)*
*Brooklands CP School*


## RED ROSES, PINK FLOWERS IN THE HOT SUMMER GIAD

I woke up, the sun was shining through the window
Flowers growing red and yellow
Summer roses through my bedroom window
Birds whistling in the treetops
Everyone shouting, I don't know why
I can smell the fresh bread coming from downstairs.

*It must be me!*

*Lauren Clarke (8)*
*Brooklands CP School*

# WAR AND PEACE

War is a brutal beast
Destroying everything in its path.
Peace is a gentle bluebird
Spreading joy everywhere.
As the monstrosity of the evil demon spreads
The fires of Hell.
We kill and hunt for blood
Like a pack of wolves.
As the raging dragon's fire
Dwells inside of us
Reviling the monster we are.

War is a bloody battle
As the hounds guard the bubbling blood stew
Like witches do.
Peace is beautiful
And peaceful.
War is a dangerous game
Played by fools
With blood, sweat and murder.
Will this world never cease?
Or will evil prevail?

*Chandini Chuni  (10)*
*Brooklands CP School*


## SNOW

Beautiful birds looking for food
People throwing snowballs at each other
Clouds flowing across the sky
People putting nuts and seeds out for the birds
Dark smoke coming out of lovely houses
Mums and dads all wrapped up warm
Everyone running to shops

Supermarkets overflowing with people
Birds all over the bird tables
Girls singing happily in the snow
Snow falling in enormous flakes
Snow all over the place
Cars sliding all over the place

*Aaron Shaw  (9)*
*Brooklands CP School*


## MY ROOM

The clock has struck midnight,
It's the time when toys come out to play.

When the teddies come out to play,
They play on a toy wooden sleigh.
The racing cars zoom in my big room.
Swirling round my chairs,
Going under my cupboard door,
Around wooden blocks,
And other toys.
The dolls are building trucks out of Lego,
And other construction toys.
One of them was putting on the wheels.
The robots are having a fight,
In a wrestling ring
With eyes flashing off and on,
Red and blue,
And blue robot won the fight.

*Andrew Webb  (7)*
*Brooklands CP School*

## WAR AND PEACE

War is a dreadful place to be,
With its horrors and spooks,
Just like a ghost chasing you.
Peace is a nice, quiet place,
Where you can feel happy to be,
With no bombs and no dead people lying on the street.
War is a no-man's-land with guns and terrorists.
Peace is not a no-man's-land with quiet noises
And no weapons to be seen.

Peace is like a songbird singing in the air,
Just to see nothing that kills.
War is a zone where you have to make sacrifices,
Also killing people in dark muddy trenches.
Peace is a world where no blood will drop,
War is a world where blood will spill.

War is like a hammer
Destroying everything that's in its way.
Peace is like a nail,
Making friends with everyone it meets.
War is noisy and scary,
Peace is quiet with no scary things.
So will it be war or peace?

*Li-Ke  (10)*
*Brooklands CP School*


## A STARRY NIGHT

As Van Gogh worked hard and his colours went round
And the canvas got streaks of red
And the colours became lively
Going *swish, swash* across the canvas

It's got houses and hills with is favourite colours
Blue, green, yellow, black and red
As the colours prance across the canvas
With shadows and with a swirly sky.

*Hannah Shaw (8)*
*Brooklands CP School*

## WAR AND PEACE

Peace, a graceful swan,
But war, people have gone.
Sitting on those old brown benches,
While men are stuck in filthy trenches.
Beautiful birds fly overhead,
Soldiers' clothes are stained in red.

Peace is family, you and me,
War is like a sting of a bee.
Peace is restful, delightful, shy,
Peace is quiet and calm,
But war has a heartbreaking alarm.

Peace is a family feast,
War is a brutal beast.
Peace is full of laughs and games,
War is fire from Hell's flames.
When peace is around there's no need to moan,
But war is hard and tough like stone.

So now you've read this all the way through,
Have you spotted my simple clue?
Read once more and then you'll see,
That war and peace are opposites, definitely.

*Stephanie Jones (10)*
*Brooklands CP School*

# WRETCHED WAR COMPARED TO PERFECT PEACE

Peace is . . .
Like the Sugar Plum Fairy
Dancing gracefully,
With innocent, tranquil swans
Floating restfully.

War is . . .
Full of pain, guns, diseases and anger,
With dogfights crowned in flames.

Peace is . . .
A paradise full of flying doves,
With angels resting on
Peaceful, drifting clouds.

War is . . .
*Bang!*
The cage of a roaring beast clattering.
*Aaaaahhhhh!*
The screams of a plane falling
From the polluted sky.

A world of haven
Compared to the pits of Hell! . . .
A glistening rainbow
Compared to a dying member of your family! . . .

Which would you prefer! . ..

***Olivia Birchenough  (11)***
***Brooklands CP School***

# WAR AND PEACE

War is brutal and rough like stone,
Peace is gentle and couldn't break a bone.
War is an enemy and a killing machine,
Peace is joyful like a splendid dream.
War is harmful and sharp as a knife,
Peace is happiness and full of life.

War is a dreadful storm,
Peace is the birds waking you at dawn.
War is sickening and bloody,
Peace is having fun with your buddy.
War is dull and black as night,
Peace is harmless and bright as light.

War is an army of guns and knives,
Peace is a gift that saves many lives.
War is the same as failing a test,
Peace is the same as coming out best.
War is like treading on nails,
Peace is like happy ending tales.

War is a nightmare in the dark,
Peace is like a walk in the park.
War is sad, cruel and stupid,
Peace is love created by Cupid.
War is death, peace divine.
Choose peace because war's a crime.

*Ben Copeland  (10)*
*Brooklands CP School*

## WAR AND PEACE

Battle! Battle! Crash! Crash!
Fighting war, mean war.
Like a raging fire of death,
Bickering enemies, picking a fight.
Muddy trenches, shouting out loud.
Bang! Bombs! Boom! Guns!
The whistling of the bullet, cutting through the wind,
A pit of snakes, the darkness of space.

Silence . . . peace . . . quiet . . . serene.
White world, happy world,
A calm world, like a year with only sunshine as weather.
A smooth world, a whispering world,
A luxurious clan of pleasant people.
It smells of brilliant perfume,
Like a brand new car, the smell of polish,
A new house, a new life.

War is sinister, no one enjoys it,
While perfect peace is luscious, a wonderful world.
Limited down to bangs and crashes,
Satan's friend is war, smirking in the notorious folds of his cloak.
Money is like war, which rules all,
But as quiet as a mouse, peace gets the better bet.
Who wants war, its evil leer?
Everyone wants peace, its gentle touch.

*Alexander Knight  (11)*
*Brooklands CP School*

# WAR AND PEACE

War is about destruction and death,
Peace is known to be full of happiness.
The awful war is death at door,
Friends and families lives been lost,
For peace is nothing like the war,
Peace is made to help the wounded,
Make their lives live once more.

War is where people die,
Noises, alarms surround the sky.
War is one thing you wouldn't want to do,
So why did I have to,
War is when you have to see,
All the fires burning free.

Peace is kind, loyal and brave,
With a gentle breeze of joy.
Peace brings you a sense of good luck,
No fighting, no death, all houses stayed up,
Peace is Heaven and harmony,
A pinch of air is ever so clean.

Read this poem carefully,
Would you pick
Peace . . .
Or would you pick war?

*Jessica Dalby  (11)*
*Brooklands CP School*

## SUNNY SUMMER'S DAY

Today it will be scorching hot
In London, Manchester, Sale, the lot,
It will be a lovely day for the seaside
To see the shiny, glistening tide.
24°C it will be today
A good time in the silky, soft sand to play.
To shadow you take a sunshade,
Don't forget your sunscreen and lemonade.

It will be scorching hot today,
I can tell you that - hip, hip hooray.

I'm sorry to say there might be a shower,
I can say this, it won't come down with power.
There will be seagulls swooping everywhere
And the sweet smell of fresh air.
There will be pebbles shining in the sun
And crabs nibbling at your bun.
Sweet tasting, salty sea
Sand in your cup of tea!

It will be scorching hot today,
I can tell you that - hip, hip hooray.

Make sure you leave soon after one,
Because you're going to lose your favourite sun.
There will be wind and rain,
Rain, that big pain.

*Jenny Brocklebank  (9)*
*Brooklands CP School*

## THE SEASONS

In the spring there's blazing heat,
Especially in Crête.
There will be fully grown trees,
And lots of bumblebees.
The birds with wing,
It happens in spring.

In the summer everything is busy,
But you might get quite dizzy.
The summer is also hot,
As boiling as a pot.
Days are long,
Your alarm clock goes pong.

In the autumn it's getting cold,
Not many people are bold.
The leaves start to fall,
Stop the ball.
Everyone stops playing,
And stops everything.

In the winter it's also cold,
Some animals become old.
And it really snows,
You also lose your bows.
The snow is freezing,
Just like your freezer.

*Husain Mohammad (8)*
*Brooklands CP School*

## WAR AND PEACE

War is a vomiting volcano
Burning past the sun,
Slashing out at everything in its path,
Killing everyone.

Peace is soft, a cool tropical ocean,
A beautiful, luxurious glen,
The blazing white sun flaming on the beach,
Warm and quite, your own special den.

War is an army of evil hounds
Guarding a sizzling, bubbling pit of blood,
A giant swamp monster lurks beneath
The smelly, dirty lake of mud.

Peace is like the smell coming from the bakery
Making a warm toffee cake,
Iced with chocolate fudge, and cream
Finished off with a marzipan flake.

So remember this poem,
You've got to be sure,
Should you pick peace . . .
Or should you pick war?

*Daniel Kettle  (10)*
*Brooklands CP School*


## VAN GOGH - STARRY NIGHT

How I wish I could have seen Van Gogh's paints
Leaping, twisting, turns and curls of paint
He made his picture look so real
He worked so hard without even a meal

He smudged the colours blue and green
Such exciting work you have ever seen
He painted Starry Night with such light
The silvery glow of the moon is a wonderful sight.

*Imogen Brownlee (8)*
*Brooklands CP School*

## WAR AND PEACE

War is a mad volcano erupting, destroying everything in its path.
War is a devastating time for people,
Bombs falling from the sky,
Golden fires and explosions,
People dying in pain,
Dripping with blood.

Peace is soft,
A cool, tropical ocean,
A beautiful country cottage,
The smell of a bakery,
Warm and quiet, restful and calm.

War is an enemy of hounds,
Guarding prisoners,
In dirty dark cells,
War is a death field,
With dirty trenches,
And a bulldozer tearing up peace.

Peace is beautiful,
Songbirds singing,
And sitting on park benches,
War is very destructive,
But peace will go on forever.

*Jack Cadman (11)*
*Brooklands CP School*

## A LOVELY SUMMER'S MEADOW

One summer's day we decided to go to the summer's meadow
and this is what happened.

The chirping birds in the meadow
The cool breeze beside you
Fluttering butterflies on your shoulder
What could be more pleasant?

The buzzing bees in the meadow
The warm sunlight on your face
Rustling leaves around you
The trees swaying
What could be more pleasant?

Colourful flowers in the meadow
The wind spinning everywhere
My summer jacket with wind in it
What could be more pleasant?

We're running through the grass
Singing as we may
No one to tell us off anymore
What could be more pleasant?

*Sophia Lapczynsky  (9)*
*Brooklands CP School*


## THE THUNDERSTORM IS HERE

The clouds cover up the shining moon
Lights are going to flicker very soon.
Adults calming children down
The thunderstorm should soon calm down.

Candles are the only good light
This is a very creepy night.
The wind is howling like a dog
Nothing like a gentle frog.

Thunder's roaring in the air
Everybody has a scare.
Sky is booming everywhere
What's that howling? It might be a bear.

Babies are crying in the cots
What's that burning? It feels hot.
This is a typical thunderstorm
Phew! There's light, it's almost dawn.

**Ben Daniels  (9)**
**Brooklands CP School**


## RAIN, FROST AND SNOW

I was lying in my bed on a snowy morning.
When I went outside I could feel the snow when I picked it up.
I could hear the spangles of rain falling to the ground.
My mum went in the car and she couldn't see a thing
Because the car was icy.
My mum could not go out in it.

*Weather News*
It is frosty in the north east of Manchester
A little bit of rain in London
Traffic trouble in Devon
And it might frost and flood in Cornwall and Glasgow
Rain in the north east of Glasgow
So be warned
Rain in Manchester and floods
And any more news will be put on the website or teletext.

**Fay Gregg  (8)**
**Brooklands CP School**

## MY BUSY TOY SHOP

The clock on the wall has struck midnight,
It's time when toys come out to play.

The bears are having a birthday party,
They're really enjoying themselves.
They've got a big birthday cake,
They're blowing candles all about
And having such fun.

The Beanie Babies are having trouble,
Of what they're going to play.
They're thinking and winking,
It is dreadfully hard.

The dolls are having a picnic,
They're eating all sorts of things.
There are cakes and drinks,
It does look nice.

*Ruqaiyah Kosser (7)*
*Brooklands CP School*


## RAIN NEVER GOES

There will be heavy showers coming in from the west.
You will need a woolly jumper and leggings and some wellies.
There will be soggy mud and heavy rain showers.
You will get heavy breezes and you will be quite chilly.
You will find heavy showers coming in from the east.
There will also be wet leaves.
And it will be 17 degrees.

*Katie Ann Worsencroft (9)*
*Brooklands CP School*

## THE NIGHT THE TOYS CAME TO LIFE

The clock on the wall has struck midnight,
It's time for the toys to come out to play.

The panda is playing on the carpet
He is trying to make a perfect castle,
But he can't seem to build the bricks up right again
Because he knocked it over.

The bears are having a boxing match
And Big Bear is winning,
Middle Size Bear is not happy
And Little Bear is crying his eyes out.

The football figures are having a football match
And some of them are fighting,
Some of them are out
Because they are hurt.

*Eleanor Downing  (7)*
*Brooklands CP School*


## TOYS ALIVE

The clock on the wall has struck midnight
It's the time when toy robots come out to play.
The toy robots are watching Power Rangers on TV
Now it has finished so the toy robots are flashing their eyes
Like they are like mad
The cars out zooming round the track
And crashing into lamp posts
Going crazy like Gimbze and fast round the track
And going mad.

*Sarah Carroll  (6)*
*Brooklands CP School*

## MY ROOM

The clock on the wall has struck midnight,
It's the time the toys come out to play.

The panda is painting a picture
With lots of people in the day.
The bears are having a disco,
The fat one has taken off his socks.
The cars are zooming down the track,
One of the cars has lost his wheel.
The other one has lost his racing hat.
Harry Potter is flying his broomstick.
Oh yes! He has won.
Now he gets the trophy
And he is eating a chocolate frog.
The David Beckham figure has kicked it in Ryan Giggs' face
And Andy Cole has scored a hat-trick
And the fans are all cheering
With red and white hats.
Night's over.
The clock struck seven -
They tidy and sweep up the floor
And by nine they're just toys in a toy shop
With an open sign up on the door.

*Charlie Bergmann  (7)*
*Brooklands CP School*


## A STARRY NIGHT

Dramatic movements
Swinging movements
Swishing movements
Waving movements
Scary movements
A frieze of colour

Dash of red
Dash of blue
Dash of yellow
Dash of green
Dash of black.

*William Weir  (8)*
*Brooklands CP School*


## MONET'S WATER LILIES

M  y garden, nice and big
O  ver the bridge I go
N  icely skipping all around, through the trees I go
E  xcellent, looking up in the sky, nearly falling in
T  he pond is very clean
S  lowly my skip turns to a jog

W  ater suddenly turns fast and makes me jump
A  nd I've fallen in the rushing water
T  he water rushing past my soaking clothes
E  very time I swoop past the side I try to grip on but - I can't
R  acing through the water,

L  ooking from side to side
I  still can't grab on
L  ook here comes my friends, look, they're coming to help me out.
I  shout, 'Help.' Here they come
E  asily they pull me out
S  houting, 'Here we come.'

*Imogen Jones  (7)*
*Brooklands CP School*

## TOYS ALIVE

The clock on the wall has struck midnight
It's the time when toys come out to play.

The Beanie Babies are talking about what they could do
Then one Beanie Baby said, 'Let's go to the animal zoo.'

The cuddly toys came out of the washing machine
And did you know they were clean
Then, dripping wet, they went to bed.

The dolls are making a castle with blocks and bricks
They have finished it now
They have got a raffle in the kitchen.

The cars are going crazy
Then racing round the room
I think they're going wild
And each has got a broom.

*Rachel Jeffree  (6)*
*Brooklands CP School*


## STARRY NIGHT

Look at the swirling stars at night
And I think you might be right
Vincent Van Gogh's painting, Starry Night
He paints each day, all day
In a colourful, energetic way
He did this without any pay
His crazy brushstrokes were quick and fast
His twirling marks were made to last.

*Abigail Parmeshwar  (8)*
*Brooklands CP School*

## My Toy Shop

The clock on the wall has struck midnight,
It's the time when the toys come out to play.

The bears are reading,
They are playing,
One thing, they were painting.
The panda was having a wedding
And they were colouring a picture of the panda.
And the dolls were making a book
With paper and sticks
And they were having a birthday party
With a cake and a balloon.
And the night is over
And inside the sign says open again.

*Megan Johnstone (6)*
*Brooklands CP School*


## Toys Alive

The clock on the wall has struck midnight
It's the time when toys come out to play.

The Beanie Babies are having a ride on the cuddly toys
And others are climbing away
At the K-nex they built
The last ones are all having a race
On the car's track.
But what's this?
The football figures are watching the TV.
The FA Cup Final is on!
We're sat on a leather settee
With a widescreen TV having fun.

*Connor Bartlett (7)*
*Brooklands CP School*

## I Love My Toys

The clock on the wall has struck midnight.
It's time when the toys come out to play.

The stretch ants stretch around the room.
The cuddly bumblebee hums about.
The cat crawls about and miaows a lot
To wake up the rest of the toys.
Dippy duck is dipping her head in her pond.
The juggler is doing his tricks
And all the toys want to see
So they get up behind him.
Night is over, the clock's ticking seven.
They tidy and sweep up the floor
And now they're just toys in a toy shop.

*Cynthia Emeagi  (6)*
*Brooklands CP School*


## My Room

The clock on the wall has struck midnight,
It's time when toys come out to play.

My furry snake was teasing my fish
The snake kept pretending to put food in their tank.
Action Man kept firing the potato gun in Doctor X's face
And he went *ooouuu*
When he kept on getting splatted in the face.
The Thunderbirds flying all over the place
Rescuing people everywhere.
My bear making buns
And giving them to the other teddies and customers.

*Luke Tatton  (6)*
*Brooklands CP School*

## THE TOY SHOP

The clock on the wall has struck midnight.
It's the time when toys come out to play.

The robots and Action Men and all the other toys.
The robots are marching all over
And having a great parade
Flashing their eyes, shaking the shelves
And having the best time.

The Action Men are practising acrobats
They're doing amazing back flips
They're winning gold medals and cups
Standing on stage with all the crowd.

*Jack Nealon  (7)*
*Brooklands CP School*


## WATER LILIES

W   atch those plants swaying in the wind
A   nd I can feel the cold wind blowing against my face
T   hey fan across the bridge, oh no! They're going to fall in
E   asily I pull them out
R   ound I go, all wet and soggy

L   ong trails through the winding stream
I   pass through the woods
L   ook left, look right
I   see a shadow, it flicks
E   asily I sprint after
S   uddenly I catch it, it's a mouse.

*Joshua Redman  (7)*
*Brooklands CP School*

## MONTY'S INCREDIBLE JOURNEY

Into a dark hedge,
Across a big garden,
Under a smelly load of rubbish,
Against a rusty fence,
Over a wooden old Wendy house,
Through a colourful passageway,
Past a mega old tree,
Between a beautiful set of flowers,
Upon a shiny bridge,
Beyond a patch of swishing grass,
After a drizzling river,
Beneath a golden aeroplane flying up above,
Beside a broken down school,
Around a twirly, whirly swing,
And at last he reached home,
Very puffed out - but happy.

*Laura Temperley (7)*
*Brooklands CP School*


## STARRY NIGHT

Twirling, swirling, starry sky.
Crashing, bashing, starry night.
Whizzing, blurry, the nights get cold.
Vibrating colours all go by.
Dramatic movements in the sky.
Now it's time to say goodbye.

*Emma Jones (8)*
*Brooklands CP School*

## MONTY'S INCREDIBLE JOURNEY

Into a wet patch of mud and slime
No water in sight
Across a wet valley full of soil, mud and slime
Under a slippery slab of pebbles
Against a gigantic tree stump
Over a spooky gate of wood
Through the damp patch of muddy grass
Past the thundering thunderstorm
Between two running birds
Ready to pounce upon a broken gate
Beyond his safe place of his health
Beside a battered birds nest with broken eggs
Around a hill so steep and bad hill it is
And at last he reached home
Very puffed out - but happy.

*Freya Dew  (8)*
*Brooklands CP School*


## STARRY NIGHT

I was sitting on a bench
I looked all ways
I looked up to the inky sky
The stars were shining mad
I wish I could have seen Van Gogh
I wish, I wish I had
Did you know he cut his ear off?
Oh that wasn't very good.
He used his pictures with so much texture
If you rubbed your hands down it
It's like a cheese grater.

*Abigail Windle  (8)*
*Brooklands CP School*

## MONTY'S INCREDIBLE JOURNEY

Into a slimy gutter,
Across the watery seas,
Under some squelchy mud,
Against the stony wall,
Over the slippery tar,
Through an echoing tunnel,
Past the black cave,
Between two big rocks,
Upon some spiky leaves,
Beyond his old mouse hole,
After the clattering rain,
Beneath the big boulder,
Beside falling grit,
Around a big hole,
And at last he reached home
Very puffed out - but happy.

*Stuart Heywood  (7)*
*Brooklands CP School*


## STARRY NIGHT

As swirling painted stars in the night
I hope you are right
With curling and twirling and whooshing and swooshing
All in a frosty night
This wonderful painting by Van Gogh
Is floating and winding and hissing and twirling
All in one winter's night.

*Jennifer Edmonds  (7)*
*Brooklands CP School*

## MONTY'S INCREDIBLE JOURNEY

Into the dark and the old forest
Across a horrible dark ditch
Under a lot of trees that had hardly any leaves
Against an old ruin
Over a table that had no legs
Though a dungeon that was dark and smelly
Past a very rust gate with only one hinge
Between two weeping willows
Upon the stinky river with lots of toads
Beyond a big, long field
After a huge log that was covered in mud
Beneath a massive tree
Beside him were two large rocks
Around him were two fat cats
And at last he reached home
Very puffed out - but happy.

*Joe Mather  (7)*
*Brooklands CP School*


## BUBBLES

Bubbles float up.
Bubbles are colourful.
Bubbles float in the sky.
They float to me.
They go up and down.
In the night they shine.
Bubbles look like planets.
Bubbles look like a rainbow.

   *Pop! Pop!*

*Alexandra Boocock  (6)*
*Brooklands CP School*

## MONET'S GARDEN

M y mum says I can go out today
O utside I go
N ow the fun has begun
E very bird I see in the sky I
T ry to catch but they're too high
S tretching footsteps I make as I creep up behind a butterfly

G ot you! I caught it
A aah! I've fallen in
R ippling water carries me down the river
D rowning I thought
E verywhere seems blue
N o, I couldn't be drowning because I can swim!

*James Milton  (8)*
*Brooklands CP School*


## MONET'S GARDEN

Mind the nettles and the spiky bushes.
Oh dear my foot is stuck in the bridge.
Now I fall in the pond, friends help me.
Admittedly my friends jump in but they can't swim.
Treading water, trying to climb up on the grass.
Slowly I get out of the pond.
Blazing sun on the lilies
A water beetle's making sounds.
Red sunlight in the sky.
Dazzling lilies floating
With elegant frogs jumping around.

*Sam Hyde  (8)*
*Brooklands CP School*

## MONET'S GARDEN

M onet's garden is really pretty in summer
O ne day I went there
N ow let me tell you what happened
E verything was silent
T ill we got bored
S o then we started to give each other dares

G ary dared me to start running about like I was mad
A nd suddenly splash! I found myself in a bluey, greeny, wet place
R eally strange, though, I realised I'd fallen in
D ear oh dear, she's fallen in the water
E veryone came to pull me out
N ow will someone get me a towel?

*Caitlin Elston  (7)*
*Brooklands CP School*


## WATER LILIES

W ater like a magic mirror,
A s I walk across the bridge I see my own reflection
T hrough the bushes and round the trees
E veryone likes me to pick them flowers
R ain trickling through the leaves

L illies flowing down the stream as I watch them pass
I like going down to the water to see it slowly run
L ittle steps as I cross, look, there's my friend from next door
I sit down to watch the sunset fill the night sky
E veryone comes to join me on the bridge
S ome people go, some people stay to watch the moon come before
it's day.

*Emma Hollows  (7)*
*Brooklands CP School*

## MONET'S WATER LILIES

M onet has a garden with a bumpy bridge.
O range water lillies started to appear.
N obody had seen such nice little water lillies.
E verybody who passed by saw the wonderful sight of them.
T rees and willows.
S izzling water washing down the stream.

W ater lillies creeping up the stream.
A boy runs across the bridge
T rying to keep safe.
E very little water lily looks bright, nice.
R ipe-looking like berries on the big trees.

L ooking at the world so nice
I n the morning sunset.
L aughing people come to look at the garden.
I mpressive as it stands in the
E choing
S ilent night.

*Kate Davies  (7)*
*Brooklands CP School*


## MONTY'S INCREDIBLE JOURNEY

Into the dark, misty night
Across the muddy road
Under the swaying bridge
Against the wooden, brown fences
Over the large swing bridge
Through the massive hole in the gate
Past the dark, gloomy house
Between the banks

Upon the house roofs
Beyond the windy trees
After the dark blue sky
Beneath the sewers of houses
Beside the windy fences
Around the misty sky
And at last he reached home
Very puffed out - but happy.

*Cara Janes (7)*
*Brooklands CP School*

## MONTY'S INCREDIBLE JOURNEY

Into the dark, dark, rusty forest.
Across the rainy, wet road.
Under the old, old tunnel.
Against old chicken run.
Over the rusty big tip.
Through the wet cornfield.
Past the pig, old pig sty.
Between the big, noisy zoo and the old smelly farm.
Upon the old, old, rusty houses.
Beyond the big, old, fishy sea.
After the duck pond.
Beneath the old, creaky gate.
Beside the old postbox.
Around the footstep
And at last he reached home
Very puffed out - but happy.

*Andrew Hamilton (7)*
*Brooklands CP School*

## MONET'S GARDEN

M any children are rushing by along the side of the gushing water.
O nly me is sat by the pool smelling the pretty rows.
N aughty Jake picked some flowers.
E veryone runs along the bridge playing catch.
T inkling bluebells are dinging by.
S inging birds are flying by and have landed on the bridge.

G anging round and chasing the multicoloured butterfly.
A hh, I've just fallen, teacher comes to pick me up.
R unning faster, faster, running, out of breath - stop!
D ancing along the riverbank with primroses in our hair.
E nding the fun with a song on the bridge.
N ever, in fact, always come again, look, look left.

*Grace Watson (7)*
*Brooklands CP School*


## MONET'S GARDEN

M aking mud splash everywhere
O pen spaces in the air
N ettles pinching, pinging me
E vergreen growing on a very tall oak
T rees swaying, swishing and tickling me
S uddenly I fell in

G rabbing plants in the whooshing stream
A lex, my favourite friend, ran to try and help
R aining, hiding under the weeping willow
D emon leaves feel like demons
E very friend helps another
N o one said one friend can't help another.

*Samantha Walters (7)*
*Brooklands CP School*

## MONET

M onet has a marvellous garden
O ld Monet was a brilliant artist
N ow he experimented with colour and light
E very day he loved to paint is water lillies
T ogether with his wife, Alice, he raised eight children
S omehow Monet became very popular

G reat colours all over
A great painter he is
R olling dashes all over the pond
D ashes are the best bit of all his painting
E xciting colours all over the place
N ow it's all the light!

*Michael English  (7)*
*Brooklands CP School*


## MONET'S GARDEN

M onet's garden
O f bright, shiny sun
N ight and day, it's still beautiful
E veryone loves Monet's garden
T ell that it's good
S ailing on the pond

G arden, oh how beautiful
A flower on the grass
R aining, you get wet
D o go there, oh it's the best!
E ven the bridge is good
N ext time, well take your paints!

*Aymen Alshawi  (7)*
*Brooklands CP School*

## WINTER

Winter comes
When the birds start singing
Into the winter breeze.

Winter comes
When the frost is coming
And the cars are frosting.

Winter comes
When the people start
Getting warmer then colder.

Winter comes
When the snow and rain
Starts coming.

Winter comes
When the animals stop
Crowing, they start hibernating.

*Ryan Hession  (8)*
*Brooklands CP School*


## BUBBLES

Bubbles go up and down
And in the dark they look like planets in the night.
When they are ready to pop
They come to me and they pop
And they glide to me
When they fly to me
And pop on me.
Sometimes they pop on the ground.

   *Pop!*

*Helena Wright  (5)*
*Brooklands CP School*

## WATER LILIES

W ater lilies, water lilies, sparkling in the sun
A hh so sensational
T winkling in the spring
E nter with a shock
R osy, A for autumn

L earn the wonder
I magine to be there
L ovely all the time
L uxury Monet
I love him so much
E ven in the evening, so beautiful
S hadow in the night.

*Ashley Cleary (8)*
*Brooklands CP School*

## THE BUBBLES

They have a rainbow inside the bubbles.
You can get small bubbles
Or you can get big bubbles.
They pop if something touches it.

They were small bubbles
When they came to me.
They pop, they go up and down.
I like bubbles.
I like to blow them.

   *Pop!*

*Hope Weir (6)*
*Brooklands CP School*

## WATER LILIES

W ater glistens, water floats.
A rtists splash and dribble the paint.
T he light and colour twinkle like stars.
E mpty paint pots littered his studio.
R unning under the Japanese bridge are lily ponds.

L ily ponds float and shiver in the sun.
I vy grows up the side behind the bridge.
L isten, you can hear the birds.
I 'll hope to see the swirling leaves tomorrow.
E veryone likes Monet's paintings.
S ee for yourself at Giverny.

*Katie Higgins  (7)*
*Brooklands CP School*


## EVENING

Evening comes when I come home from boring working.
Evening comes when I am changing.
Evening comes when we are eating.
Evening comes when I am playing.
Evening comes when we are *scaring!*
Evening comes when I am tiring.
Evening comes when we are cleaning.
Evening comes when I am reading.
Evening comes when we are *snoring!*
Evening comes when owls are hooting.

*Ross Atkinson  (9)*
*Brooklands CP School*

## FORECAST

Welcome to tonight's forecast
It'll be cold in the north west.
There may be a few showers
That might affect the lawn mowers.
Quite so many warns
About the heavy, heavy storms.
Then a bit of southern light
And a much warmer Fahrenheit.
The temperature is a bit cool
But then not for a mule
And there comes morning bright
Then evening night.

*Tejal Patel  (9)*
*Brooklands CP School*


## MONET'S GARDEN

Monet's garden is the best in the world
Water smooth in the day
And the sun plays on the water
The leaves on the trees are yellow, pink and reds
They are the best
And they are nice
So come, it is at Giverny
Please, please come to Monet's garden
As nice as can be
It is nice and good
So please come to Monet's garden.

*Henry Naylor  (7)*
*Brooklands CP School*

## FRED BLOKES

There once was a boy called Fred Blokes
Whose habit was cracking bad jokes.
He sat down to dine
And got along fine
Until folks
Got bored with his jokes.

He was born in the town of Dundee
Then he said it was up to me
To help those folks
To crack a few jokes
And they were so rotten
They forgot 'em.

Now one was 'bout a bunny
And he thought it was awfully funny
He told an old bloke
This rubbish old joke
After that he cried
Then he died.

*Sam Hughes  (9)*
*Brooklands CP School*

## MONET'S GARDEN

M   onet's garden in Giverny is very beautiful
O   ver the lily pond stands the Japanese bridge
N   o one leaves disappointed
E   very visitor is very happy to see Monet's garden
T   ourists love Monet's use of light and colour.

*Emily Hough  (7)*
*Brooklands CP School*

## TAKE THE BATH, BILL

A boy called Bill never took a bath
He thought it was such a big laugh

He stinks so much and smells
No one plays with him unless the teacher tells

So Bill, the boy who never took a bath
Really thought it was a big laugh

He knew he would get smelly
Especially when he smells his belly

Though the boy called Bill still never took the bath
So happy he took it as one big laugh

He then decided to take it and then found out
The taps ran out.

*Daniel Fisher  (9)*
*Brooklands CP School*


## ONE HOT SUMMER'S DAY

There is going to be a fantastic summer's day
And it is going to be 30°
And at night-time I think it will be 10°
But I don't think I will feel it because I have got central heating
But one night when I went down to check on my dog
To see what he was doing
All I could see in my eyes was sparkle.

*Kerry Anne  (8)*
*Brooklands CP School*

## BONFIRE NIGHT

A damp, cold night is waiting for the fiery beast to appear
The rain is spitting down on our faces
The people are covered from head to toe in warm clothing
The sky is empty and goes on forever
Suddenly the fire was lit

It crackles and spits into the air
Roaring like a hungry lion
Ready to pounce on its unsuspecting prey
Its forked fiery tongues lick the cold night air
And devours the cardboard and wood
It breathes out a breath of cardite smoke
And settles down to its flaming depths

Whizz, bang, rockets shooting into the air
Like a plate of gold scattering its jewels
It stands out like an illuminated shooting star
On the ebony black sky
The Catherine wheel whizzing round like a shower of diamonds

The crowds drift away
The hungry dragon falls away
Quietness reigns again
Darkness returns again
Suddenly the coldness returns to the night again.

*Ben Winby (11)*
*Brooklands CP School*


## FROSTY MORNINGS

I wake up in the morning
Go turn on the TV
The forecast says you'll be lucky
If you don't just freeze.

So the forecast says it's frosty
But I don't really care
I've got my hood and mackintosh
And I'm playing in the air.

*Gareth Williams  (8)*
*Brooklands CP School*


## WAR AND PEACE

War is a whirlwind tearing our world
Snatching the people's blood, guts and all
Peace is a halo that brightens our lives
Walking along the sweet, silver skies.

War is a volcano bursting to kill
Crawling across with its full-powered drill
Joy is the key to Heaven
Heaven is a sweet paradise.

*Bang!* Is the sound that they will hear last
Screaming and shouting as they take a last gasp
A calm tropical ocean lies quiet, still
As a swift, serene swan takes a dip.

The massive murderous gun takes one shot
As pain soars the world with a weeping cry
Out pops a baby with an innocent smile
The joyous white dove coos for its love.

People dying, people smiling
    Dying      Smiling
    Dying      Smiling

Which do you prefer?

*Laura Heywood  (11)*
*Brooklands CP School*

## THE BOOMING BONFIRE

A terribly cold night,
Awaits the arrival of the hot, bright bonfire,
It's so cold,
It's like being put into a freezer,
The dark sky is waiting for all the colourful fireworks,
The cold rain starts to spit into all the spectators' faces,
People are dressed in many layers with hats, gloves and scarves,
Eventually the great gorilla is lit.

Shining and crackling,
The hairy gorilla awakes,
Reaching for its unaware prey,
Higher and higher the gorilla grasps,
Like a person trying to change a light bulb,
Finally with its tongue it grabs its prey,
Floating down the beast with its prey,
Is mouth full with cordite breath.

Screaming, noisy rockets shoot into the air,
Like a shooting star whizzing across the Earth,
An eagle shoots up with my eyes fixing on it,
Shiny, sizzling, sparklers illuminate the dull sky.
Buzz . . . the Catherine wheel shoots round like an active chainsaw,
Fountains of rubies spurt out of the firework.

Spectators wander home,
The big gorilla has eaten his fill,
The monster calms his nerves and goes to sleep,
The gorilla slowly dies away,
Flints and ash blow out of sight,
Silence and blackness comes at last,
To leave the damp, litter-filled ground.

*Rorie Sparkes (11)*
*Brooklands CP School*

# THE WORLD OF THE DRAGON

The cold, dark night is heading our way,
The stars are like cubic zirconium jewels
Sparkling like sizzling sparklers,
Rain is falling down,
It's so cold like snowflakes,
Groan! The dragon awakes,
Everyone slowly is getting warmer.

I see the dragon waving his fiery flames
The world can see his bright breath
As it grows and grows, never-ending,
His wings wrap around his body
Before shooting out for a fly,
Licking his tongues of flames,
The hungry beast enjoys his dinner of wood,
Calming down, his smoky breath simmers,
In a cloud of dark black ash and smoke.

Whoo! The rocket zooms past like a shooting star
In the midnight sky,
Bang! The jewels burst out of their shell,
Amusing all the people around,
Super sparkling sparklers crackling all the time,
The sky is as black as ebony, lit by the glowing jewels.

The dragon is getting tired,
He needs a nap until next year,
Food below has slowly disappeared into ash,
The jewels disappear into the velvet night,
Pitter-patter, the raindrops drizzle, falling down,
As the darkness of the sky slowly returns.

*Gabriella Farrell (10)*
*Brooklands CP School*

## MONET'S GARDEN

M any people cheering me on.
O h how am I going to get back?
N ow where did the butterfly go?
E verybody cheers as I climb onto the bridge.
T errible thoughts of me falling in.
S tep by step I lose my grip.

G rabbing at the butterfly and losing grip.
A cross the lake I swim for safety.
R aging water attracts my friends.
D ashing their quickest, they see me sinking.
E veryone cheers for my friends.
N ever stopping, they pull me free.

*Chudi Emeagi (7)*
*Brooklands CP School*


## SPARKLING, COLD SNOW

When it's snowy I would say it's going to be blowy
O now I can feel snow
The snow is falling, it's getting very cold
Now it's coming to lunchtime at twelve o'clock
My mum said, 'Be careful, you might slip on the ice.'
I tell you what, I slipped a lot
The grass is crunchy, the leaves are crackling
And my feet are very cold
There are bits of snow everywhere.

*Tim Wormald (8)*
*Brooklands CP School*

## VERY COLD WINTER'S DAY

On a very cold morning
I look out my window
And all I can see is snow, snow, snow
I open my window
And I can hear all the birds sing
It is very frosty and slippy
And there is icicles on the house
And the icicles dripped and dropped all day
And you can see and hear all the robins
And all the roots were covered in snow as well
And the trees
It will be very damp and wet in all the snow.

*Jack Smallshaw  (8)*
*Brooklands CP School*


## EVENING

When evening comes the sun is dying
Evening comes when the moon is rising
Evening comes when the trees are swaying
Evening comes when the wind is roaring
Evening comes when the squirrels are scurrying
Evening comes when the birds are sleeping
Evening comes when the lights are fading
Evening comes when I am sleeping.

*Daniel King  (9)*
*Brooklands CP School*

## BONFIRE NIGHT

A freezing cold night,
Awaits the arrival of the bonfire,
An empty sky echoes the hushed voices
Out comes the man with the blowtorch,
Everyone goes silent, holding their breath,
Suddenly the fire is lit.

Jumps up suddenly like a wild beast,
Roaring and surging, rocking with anger,
Cordite breath like mist hanging in the damp air,
Spitting brightly coloured embers like a dragon's breath,
Swallowing paper and wood for its meal,
Shooting up flames like a red-hot rocket,
Catching its prey in flight,
The hungry monster slowly dies down,
Full up, he softly calms down,
To sleep in its black, sooty, ash bed.

*Bang! Crash! Boom!*
Red-hot rockets screaming through the thick foggy air,
Golden Catherine wheels spinning like a crown of jewels,
Traffic lights bursting out like a jack-in-a-box,
Sizzling sparklers light up the night,
Although the night is nearly over the magic will never stop.

Tired people wander home,
The wild beast dies down away,
The sky is ebony black again,
Ash and soot drift around the cold night air,
Quiet and darkness returns, as the ashes drift down to the ground.

*Gavin Dixon  (11)*
*Brooklands CP School*

## THE PARTY OF THE BONFIRE

As people arrive at the quiet, restful bonfire,
The freezing, jet-black, cold night awaits them,
The cold air was like being put in a freezer,
People dressed in warm clothes gather around,
Silently waiting and waiting,
Suddenly the bonfire is lit.

The fire is like a dragon just woken up from a long annual sleep,
The rain was spitting sharply,
Flames rose up like a shivery snake,
As the dragon's food of wood and cardboard is consumed,
Becoming as colourful as a rainbow,
As the crackling comes to an end,
The dragon becomes sleepy, lying down
Upon a soft bed of sooty ashes.

Bang, crash, bang!
Noisy rockets shoot up into the velvet sky,
Catherine wheels rotate round like golden balls of fire,
Sizzling, simmering sparklers are lit,
They brighten up the dark, ebony night,
Roman candles burst up fast, spitting out golden jewels of light,
While traffic lights change colours of the rainbow,
Whizzing up from the damp, cold ground.

The crowds slowly drift away,
As the last fireworks finish,
The silence is like a night-time echo,
Once the dragon has eaten his fill,
It is time for him to go,
Everybody has to wait for yet another year.

*Charlotte Brownlee (11)*
*Brooklands CP School*

## BONFIRE NIGHT

An empty sky.
Spectators come to watch the bonfire.
Chatting voices are as noisy as a lion's roar.
Out comes the man with his blowtorch.
Everyone goes silent.
Suddenly the fire is lit.

There is a pet dragon in my garden.
Climbing up and using his flame-thrower mouth.
Burning and sizzling and cooking his food.
A bin lorry coming round eating boxes and paper.
Its hands reaching higher and higher.
Getting hungry, it starts to feed.
Swallowing wood, boxes and paper.
He has had his fill and is ready for bed.

Bang, crackle, boom.
Golden birds flying into the sky.
Shattering like a broken heart full of rubies.
Shooting up like shooting stars.
Catherine wheels spinning like a rainbow-coloured drill.
The sky becomes a picture of colour.

Tired people wander away.
The dragon dies.
The grass is ebony like the ground after a forest fire.
The sky is silent and the grass is soaked.
As the rain falls down all you can hear is the wind.

*Oliver Janes  (10)*
*Brooklands CP School*

## WAR AND PEACE

Peace is a delicate dove
Sailing over the calm, cool sea
War is a knife, a sharp, killing knife
Out to illuminate kindness and love
Peace is the halo over an angel's sparkling hair
Glowing as she plays a song on her golden harp
But beware of war
War is hunger and suffering as death takes over

Peace is a swan on a deep dark lake
As the sun dances over her tranquil feathers
Ashes are all that is left of the harmony we once had
War destroyed it . . . War destroyed our hearts

Peace is a cloud sweeping over your body
As your head lies on a deserted island
Satan's wolves never rest!
They're howling to be set free,
Howling to ruin lives,
Howling to start a war!

Yet peace is a monkey, quiet and serene
His cheeky face pokes out from the trees
War is like a raging storm
Ripping up trees and tearing down houses
Ruining lives never to be replaced.

War will turn on you
But peace will stay with you
*Forever.*

*Genevieve Riley (10)*
*Brooklands CP School*

# WAR AND PEACE!

War is the thing that can take a person's life,
A sharp, pointy, dangerous knife,
It is an evil, mad, active, angry devil,
It is horrible, a pit of Hell.

Peace is a tranquil, silver-white dove,
Peace is you and the person you love,
It's cool, relaxing music to your head,
You'll choose war, no, *peace* instead.

War is a cruel, vicious, bloody death field,
For soldiers war is a dark, silver shield,
War pierces hearts of innocent souls,
War is walking across hot coals.

Peace is as quiet as a mouse,
Searching for cheese in a big silent house,
Peace is the silence that you cannot hear,
Peace is the paradise that makes people cheer.

War is a drink of lime that is sour,
Peace is sunny as a daisy flower.
War is atrocious, cruel, harsh and . . . *bang* . . .
Peace is a place where the angels sang.

War can send down pools of fire,
Peace is angels singing in a choir,
War is like prison, not letting you free,
Peace is like spoonfuls of sugar . . . for me!

I feel that war is a raging storm,
But peace a walk though clouds, calm,
War, a place where families cry,
Peace, a place where people try.

Try to stop the war going on,
To make people live where the sun shone,
But let us pray for war never again,
It puts the people we love in pain.

So let us live in peace
Harmony too,
Because I prefer peace
Well . . . wouldn't you?

*Claire English (10)*
*Brooklands CP School*


## WAR AND PEACE

War is a beast thrashing in its cage,
A deliberate attempt to savage the world.
War chooses to destroy rather than become friends.
Tears are shed because the families' heroes have died to fight it.
Corpses lie with missing arms or limbs,
While Satan stands over them, laughing his shrill cry of victory.
*Ha, ha, ha!*
Gunfire and explosions light up the land, like the sun has settled itself
Over the body-laden battlefield.

Peace is a sign of love and friendship
On an island all alone.
A snow-white dove, graciously gliding,
To an unknown place.
A silent, desolate mountain top,
Occasionally whistling a pleasant tune.
The winding, curving road,
Leading to a deserted flower park.
Peace is a sweet, silent place.

*Nick Thomson (11)*
*Brooklands CP School*

## REMEMBER THE 5TH NOVEMBER

We excitedly await the monster in our garden.
Gathered patiently in a freezing fridge,
With a velvet-black sky with diamonds in between.
Footsteps echo as they approach us,
*Roar!*
The hungry beast awakens as the fire is lit.

Tongues of fire flicker and shine.
Rising higher and higher as the beast awakes.
Little Guy Fawkes smiling on top, the dragon's breath rising higher.
The candle wax is flaming, burning bright and hot.
Fierce and flaring the terrifying candle smokes, swallowing the wood.
Hungrily it devours all the rubbish on its high bonfire plate.

Whizzing and whistling goes the Catherine Wheel
Like a spinning ball of fire.
Crash! Whizz! Falls a fountain of shooting stars.
The rocket flies past and bang!
It bursts into jewels as colourful as a rainbow.
The sky as black as ebony with bright, blazing eyes.

The lion keeps roaring with all its might, showing its golden teeth.
It stops! Hungrily the beast eats its fill.
Pitter-patter! The rain starts to fall heavily.
The troops of spectators shuffle back home
Leaving the black ashes behind.

*Vicky Fleming  (11)*
*Brooklands CP School*

## BONFIRE NIGHT

Crowds, like a starry night, begin to pour in.
Everyone shivers and shudders in the icy black night.
The sky awaits the arrival of the fire.
Wrapped warmly like a bundle of fur.
The match is lit with jewels bombarding it.
Suddenly, out of the blue, the fire is lit.

Fire as hot as melting wax
Crawls, trying to pounce on its prey.
The dull devil's dungeon is caught alight
Howling like a dog with all his voice.
The flames lick his hungry lips.
The fire charges, gulp, gone.

Whooo, whistler whizzes up.
Rockets rush up and burst into a thousand jewels.
Sizzling sparklers, bright like the North Star.
Catherine wheels spin with scattering stars trailing behind.
Fireworks light up the dank night.
Roman candles burst like a jack-in-a-box.

Crowds begin to fade, soaked and drenched.
The finale fireworks fade into the black sheet.
Silence like a winter morning, hushed and still.
The fire beast has had his meal and falls into a deep sleep
For another year.

*Stephanie Hough (11)*
*Brooklands CP School*

# WAR AND PEACE

War is as high-pitched as a band of percussion
Peace is as soft as a cushion.
War is as bitter as a lemon
Peace is as sweet as a watermelon.

War is when men are in trenches
Peace is when women sit on garden benches.
War is as deadly as a poisonous snake
Peace is as healthy as a grape.

War is as cold as ice
Peace is as hot as boiled rice.
War is painful
Peace is unpainful.

War is when there is a stormy grey cloud
Peace is when there is a gentle, light blue sky.
War is when a tornado comes and destroys everything in its way
Peace is when you enjoy the bay.

But most of all, war will end
But peace will mend.

*So why is there war?*

**Rishabh Agrawal  (10)**
**Brooklands CP School**


# WAR AND PEACE DO NOT MIX

War is like a snake
Scaring millions,
Most men were fighting
But not the civilians,
War is like a hungry beast
While the winners have a feast.

Peace is like a park bench
Not a sword,
A shield or trench,
Peace is like a waterfall,
Calm and refreshing.
Peace is good to all,
While war is a brutal monster.

*Dominic Cole (10)*
*Brooklands CP School*

## WAR AND PEACE

War is like an angry beast soaring through the land,
Innocent English civvies holding neighbours' hands,
Peace is delightful,
Peace is rightful,
War is worthless,
Peace is precious.

People on cold park benches,
Soldiers in the muddy trenches,
Peace is calm,
War is wasteful,
Peace is careful.

War is the sharpest wire end,
Peace will be there, it is always a friend,
War is brutal,
War is cruelty.

*Peace is a blue lagoon!*

*Lucy Wood (10)*
*Brooklands CP School*

# BONFIRE NIGHT!

A freezing cold night draws in.
A stampede of elephants waiting anxiously.
The queue crawling like tiny ants.
The crowd getting bigger as the time goes by.

The sky is jet black, soon to be lit up.
People heavily dressed from the cold wind.
The noise dies down, the bonfire is lit!

The fire swirling ready to catch its prey.
Roaring like an angry beast it pounces up.
It's caught its meal.
As it breathes smoke
It surrounds the fire and hovers
Like a bird.
Acrobatic ashes fly through the sky and softly drift to the ground.

Bang! The fireworks have started.
Sparklers are lit.
Silence no more.
The eagles rush up, squealing and screeching noises are heard from
their prey.
Rainbow colours fill the sky, gold shattering, Catherine wheels,
twirling,
Screaming as they go faster!
Whoosh! Bang! Screech!
The whole sky is filled with light.

Eyes slowly pulled off the sky, people are tired, they slowly disappear.
The night is quiet once more.
The angry beast slowly drifts to sleep
And the black smoke drifts across the sky.
All the excitement is over, the night is calm, the night is asleep.

*Emma Doyle  (11)*
*Brooklands CP School*

# WAR AND PEACE

War is Satan with a black cloak,
Devil letting out his savaging bulldogs.
Peace is restful, delightful but shy,
Like the calm, deep blue sea.
War is fierce, worse than evil,
A death pit of red blood.
A gentle breeze, a choir of angels,
A tranquil paradise describes peace.

An ugly wart describes war,
A savage beast with sharp fangs.
Peace is as quiet as a sharp mouse,
The snow-white dove.
The opening jaws, the way to Hell,
Turns the sky to blood.
Peace is shy like a merry mouse,
Drifting in white, fluffy clouds.

War looks worse than the Devil's smoke,
Wolfing down innocent soldiers.
The sweet cheery cherubs singing,
Shining on a summer's day.
War is the opposite of Heaven's singing,
Like the horned red Devil.
Bang! War's brutal machines,
Wars just ready to strike.

War can end within years, but peace can live forever.

*James Hamilton (11)*
*Brooklands CP School*

## WAR AND PEACE

War is a beast, raging amongst the lands,
A deliberate attempt to gain the world,
Tears are shed for the innocent people,
Sent away to the unknown,
This insanity rules the world,
Pain and agony with it.
Gunshots and artillery light the night.
Why war?

Peace is a sign of love and tranquillity,
A snow-white dove soaring above our land.
Freedom throughout the world,
People roam free.
Friendships are formed . . . and continued.
The dark sky is ebony black and clear.
Why peace?

War rips up humanity and all that's with it,
Peace lays down new paths and new ideas.
War bulldozes future generations,
Peace is harmony and clear.

*War continues to happen but peace lives on.*

*Euan Mackway-Jones  (11)*
*Brooklands CP School*

## TOY SHOP

The pirates and the panda
Played pirates treasure hunt with Snow White.
The treasure was gold and rubies.
The robots tried to pinch the treasure.

The teddies tried to stop them by bumping into them.
The tigers were roaring as loud as they could.
The robbers jumped out of the window into a bath.
Swimming in the pool was a fish.

*James Smith  (6)*
*Brooklands CP School*


## Bonfire Night

An icy cold night
Awaits the mouthy monsters.
It's like being dipped into a big bowl of ice.
Suddenly the monsters come,
Talking,
Talking,
Talking.
The fireworks waiting to be lit.
Suddenly the bonfire is lit.

The fire is like a Chinese dragon breathing out fire.
Its eyes flicker with envy,
Its breath rising up into the dark, gloomy air.
Dancing and prancing,
Munching and crunching.
Watching the people.

Fireworks are like shooting stars, swirling and whirling,
Crafty Catherine wheels,
Racing rockets go off with a *bang!*
Sparkling sparklers glow up in the air.

It's all quiet as the crowds drift out of the gates.
At last the dragon is in peace.
Slowly the flames die off.

*Hayley White  (10)*
*Brooklands CP School*

# THE BONFIRE

The mass of people start pouring in
Like a line of ants,
They are like creepy crawlies
Slithering through the darkest night.
The beast is rousing,
It's devouring its prey.
Ready to pounce on its next victim.
As hungry as a horse,
As hot as the blazing sun.

Bright bangers shooting into the night-like sky.
It was a magical night.
Bright sparks flying through the big, black sky.

As timid as a mouse, it dies down to a crisp.
People decide to go home.
It goes dark,
There's nothing left at all.

*Hannah Sanders  (10)*
*Brooklands CP School*


# WAR AND PEACE

War is an invincible killing machine.
Peace is friendly, quiet and harmless.
War destroys anything in its path.
Peace is gentle and soft.
Unlike peace, war is an error.
Peace is as colourful as a rainbow.
War is an accident waiting to happen.
Peace is as quiet as being in a desert.
War is blood and guts.

*Joseph O'Driscoll  (10)*
*Brooklands CP School*

# WAR AND PEACE

War is like a raging fire,
It is jeopardy,
Like a gorilla trying to break out of his cage for no reason at all.

Peace is a delight and gladness,
It's the opposite to war,
It is a day in the park.

War is a paradise in Hell!
Been torched with whip, been heated in a furnace.
Endless pain.

If you fall in war you won't get back up.
And if you fall in peace there is a hand there for you.

*Lewis Clarke (11)*
*Brooklands CP School*


# SCHOOL BONFIRE

A long line of people
Waiting patiently
Suddenly the bonfire is lit
It shuffles itself up
Like a fierce dragon
Puffing and smoking like an angry beast
All of a sudden
Rockets started sparkling around
A Catherine wheel twirling and whirling
People are laughing and enjoying the bonfire and fireworks
Sparkling through the air.

*Melissa Bates (10)*
*Brooklands CP School*

# THE BONFIRE!

The people are starting to arrive,
To a wet and windy night,
The sky is black and cloudy,
People are dressed up warmly,
Ready for a cold evening,
The bonfire stands large and gloomy,
Bang! The fire is lit.

Large and fiery,
Like a dragon exploding,
The smoke reaching high in the sky,
Devouring the boxes and wood,
Slowly it begins to calm,
Until it's had its fill,
Now it sleeps until next time.

Whoosh, bang, fireworks burst,
Illuminating the night sky,
Rockets exploding like bombs,
The sky covered in mist,
Sparklers spitting sparks, spurting smoke,
Catherine wheels crackling happily.

The crowd starts to disperse,
The ashes of the fire now wet and soggy,
The air musty and smoky,
It was suddenly very quiet.

*David Robert Peckitt  (10)*
*Brooklands CP School*

## WAR AND PEACE

War is brutal
Like a beast waiting to pounce.
Peace is gentle, loving, for friends.
War is dust, killing and fighting over land.

Peace is like paradise.
Children laughing and playing with friends.
War is like a volcano erupting.
No one can escape without being killed or burnt alive.

War is bitter.
Dust like sour lemon.
While peace is like orange juice,
Not bitter but perfect.

So why are wars still going on?

*Stephen Johnson (11)*
*Brooklands CP School*

## WAR AND PEACE

War always comes at beautiful sunrise
Men are bleeding from wounds and eyes
People are dying
While families are crying

Peace is quiet, happy and calm
People holding flowers in every palm
War is cruel, nasty and sorrow
Who knows what will happen tomorrow?

Peace is like sitting on old park benches
While men are lying in muddy trenches
'Peace is today when war is tomorrow.'

*George Gallagher (11)*
*Brooklands CP School*

# BONFIRE!

A freezing cold night
The bonfire is waiting to be lit
More people are starting to arrive
Finally the bonfire is alight
Everybody feeling that their feet are coming back to life
The raging beast reaches for its prey
Hissing and spitting its way up
He is waiting fiercely
*Snap!*
The beast caught it
The beast is satisfied now he has his dinner.

Suddenly
*Bang! Boom!*
The fireworks have started
There were
Roaring rockets
Sparkling sparklers
Crazy Catherine wheels
Slowly the crowd drifts away
Whispering
'Better than last year.'
The beast is dying down
And that was the end of the bonfire.

*Jenny Hamilton (11)*
*Brooklands CP School*


# WAR AND PEACE

War is a big cloud
Peace makes us very proud.
War is like a red-hot volcano
Peace is like a beautiful rainbow.

War is like freaky dug up graveyards
Peace is like looking at your cards.
War is like a deadly poisonous snake
Peace is like a nourishing grape.

*Peter Screeton (10)*
*Brooklands CP School*

## THE BONFIRE

Tons of people pushing in the line to see the display in the dark,
smooth, plain sky
People's woolly coats brushing across children's ears
Mothers shouting for their children
Making sure they're not lost.

Waiting for everyone, a giant beast
Liquidating metals and wood
Its tongue blazing the grey smoke
Its breath like a forest fire's smoke.

Catherine wheels twizzing and spitting colours
Roman candles spraying and splurting with purple, red, gold and silver
Making loud noises like a brass band.

All the crowds seem to suddenly disappear
Everyone seemed to be weary but all of it was worth it.

*Richard Schenk (10)*
*Brooklands CP School*

## BONFIRE NIGHT

The freezing night grew
The snails arrive
Leaving echoes of parrots behind
Exciting elephants scream
For the fire to be lit
The match is ready to go
Yeah! The crowd shouts!

Crackling sticks snapping in the spitting fire
Brutal, bestial fish burning up into the night
Swimming round and round, up and up
Unaware of being an unlucky one.

Crackling Catherine wheels, spinning, shivering sparklers.
Whoosh! Crackle! Bang!
The boastful, banging, beautiful flowers blow open
Springy, sparkling sparklers
Like yellow, red, green and blue daffodils
Eyes were astonished!

Soon it reached the end
The fish grew down
And the flowers died
But the parrots came back and didn't want to leave
When they did, still like chattery chimps
The toffee apples had gone
And so were they.

*Clare Bennett (11)*
*Brooklands CP School*

## BONFIRE

A lightless cold night
People appearing from nowhere
Chatting like monkeys
The wind is howling
The dragon lies ready to wake
Suddenly he stirs.

The dragon's hungry
Torching, flaming, melting
Its unsuspecting prey
As even as the Devil
The carnage goes on
Until his hunger is satisfied.

Bang, boom, the rockets fire
Circling Catherine wheels
Roman candles shooting
As if trying to hit a far-off enemy
Sizzling, sparkling sparklers
Lighting the dull, dark night.

The crowds drift home
The dragon dies
Smoke fills the sky
Only a few survived the encounter
The dragon will live on!

*Philip Jackman (11)*
*Brooklands CP School*

## WAR AND PEACE

War is a blood lust
Which won't stop until millions are dead
Peace is a light, lofty cloud
That goes straight to the head
War is a biting blade
That the gentle shield of peace
Must fend in the shade

War is lame
When peace is sane
War slays
Peace saves
War is pain
Peace is pure
War is death but peace is life.

Remember this well
Love peace; hate war.

*James Lewis  (10)*
*Brooklands CP School*


## TOYS ALIVE

The clock on the wall has struck midnight.
It's the time when toys come out to play.
Marshmallow painted a picture of Harry Potter.
Marshmallow was covered with paint.
He tried and tried
But he coloured the picture.
He went to bed.

*Olivia Grant-Caren  (6)*
*Brooklands CP School*

## WAR AND PEACE

War is a rash that is ever following you around.
Peace is a harmless creature that locks away fights.
Blood is in every room and peace is all around you.

War is mean, as people run into burning flames just to save their people.
Peace is soft, as people get to relax all day without thoughts of
beasts roaming around.

War is monitored around the world.
The stylist light shows they have gone.
Peace is calm, a fantastic day is right as people can show lights
and get back on the road again.

*Charlotte Richards  (10)*
*Brooklands CP School*

## WAR AND PEACE

War is a big grey cloud,
Peace will make us proud,
War is like an accident about to happen,
With bombs making an enormous sound,
Peace is like a soft pillow.

War is a volcano,
Peace is a beautiful rainbow,
War is like a dug up graveyard,
Peace is looking at your birthday card.

But most of all war will end,
And peace will mend.

*Zoe Griffiths  (10)*
*Brooklands CP School*

## WAR AND PEACE

War is a bitter lemon squeezing its evil
Peace is the saviour with its white, gleaming shield
War is dreadful, casting its evil claw
Peace is white clothes with a sweet taste
Evil, black as black with its bitter perfume
Peace fighting back
Evil just waiting.

War is Hell
Peace is paradise
War, killing as it travels
Peace needing help
War overcoming it
Peace wanting allies
War does not want any.

*Tim Blower (10)*
*Brooklands CP School*


## A RABBIT

Brown and beige leaves fluttering
Dull, dark forest all muddy,
Like sinking sand.
Farmers set their bombs off
To scare birds away.
Rabbits dart through the fence
Then a fox appears from nowhere
And corners it,
Snap.
It squeals and runs down a hole.

*Adam Cosgrove (10)*
*Castle View Primary School*

## BULLYING

My socks pulled up tightly
As tough as I could be
Walking around the corner
Someone's waiting for me.
She is wearing a skirt
As short as a thumb
With plaited hair
Her blue eyes
Were staring at me
Like I was at the ocean
She scared me
So I ran around the corner
As frightened as could be.

*Toni-Lea Deane  (10)*
*Castle View Primary School*


## YEAR 6

Loud and noisy,
Quiet and shy,
Scurrying and laughing,
Pens going click!
Sam with his big mouth,
Hannah with her noises,
Karl with his snakes on the back of his chair,
Samantha with smartness,
Lyndsay falling asleep,
And I, late, late, late and late.

*Jodie Carroll  (11)*
*Castle View Primary School*

# THINGS I'D DO IF IT WEREN'T FOR THE TEACHERS

Arrive at school,
Take a long dip in the swimming pool.
Chew chewies all day long,
Have a little sing song.
Not learning anything new
Walk around in kids' spew.
Drink my Coke in music monster loud
It would feel like I was on a cloud.
Messing up the classroom
On the roof will go the broom.
No need to keep the room neat
If you're bad you'll get a treat.
Splash in puddles
Blow loads of bubbles.
Down the corridor we will rush
Not a single hush!
Enjoy lunch,
Because someone is bound to get a punch.

PS: Go to all the teachers barns,
Then raid Mrs Moore's farm.

*Hayley Holden  (10)*
*Castle View Primary School*


# SPACE

UFO spins like a roundabout
Bright orange light circling like flames
Looks like waves flashing all around
I just want to say where might he go
It is a silver ball thing, flying through the air
I don't know what shape it is but I know it is out there.

*Christopher Joyce  (11)*
*Castle View Primary School*

## ECHO

The house is swaying
Rocking, rocking.

The fence is cracking,
Breaking, breaking.

The window is dirty,
Muddy, muddy.

The sky is thundering,
Banging, banging.

The meadow still,
Silently stood.

*Emma-Lee Butterworth (11)*
*Castle View Primary School*


## WINTER

The wind was howling
And banging against the door.
The winter lasts a long time
The snow would fly side to side
And grip against my window.
The wind would blow the leaves,
The trees would blow against the floor,
The snow would be deep into the ground
And footsteps would dig in the ground.

*Steven Whitfield (11)*
*Castle View Primary School*

## THINGS I'D DO AT SCHOOL IF IT WEREN'T FOR THE TEACHERS

I'd play football all day,
With a ball made of clay.
I'd destroy the overhead,
And chop off the teacher's head.
I'd spray-paint the windows,
And destroy the spindles.
I'll eat what I want,
And do what I want,
I'd rip the comfy chairs,
And eat the teacher's teddy bears.

*David Burgess  (10)*
*Castle View Primary School*

## PASSED LIFE

I felt my tear pass my eye
When I had to say goodbye.
My heart began to break in two
When I started to miss you.
I wish you were here
Because I miss you so dear.
When we are finally reunited
I will become very excited.

*Jaimee-Lee Stacey  (10)*
*Castle View Primary School*

## OCEAN

The ocean is blue and deep
Full of seaweed covered rocks
The seals lay on those rocks as the sea rocks to and fro
The dolphins splash in and out of the water like mermaids
Under the sea the yellow butterfly fish lay.

*Lydia Jones  (10)*
*Castle View Primary School*


## UNDERNEATH THE DEEP BLUE SEA

Underneath the deep blue sea
Little yellow fish do swim
While on the other side
Great sharks are looking for their din.

Underneath the deep blue sea
Right under the splashing waves
Four little black electric eels
Were looking for their friend Dave.

Deeper underneath the sea
Right past the splashing waves
Right down upon the ocean floor
A one-eyed monster sleeps.

One eye he opens to see his prey
He is going to eat.
One slimy leg he lifts
And I can see lots of treasure
Just for me.

*Nadia Bakir  (8)*
*Davenham CE Primary School*

## TREASURE

First to the snake pit, go quick
Can you defeat the rattle snakes
Before you get to the poison lake.
If you touch the poison lake
You will sleep forever.
If you go in to the Bacardi Breeze forest
First you will become clever.
Next to jumping lava
If you fall in the lava you'll live forever.
Now to Mermaid Lagoon
Grab a balloon and go on your way
Before you get to Mountain Spray.
Go through the sky
Don't look down
And don't be a clown.
Next to Croc Pond
They'll eat people whose hair's blond.
Quick go on dig, dig
Like a pig to get the gold and silver.

*Jessica Rowlinson  (9)*
*Davenham CE Primary School*


## MR NOBODY LIVED THERE

At the top of the landing
Near the top of the stairs
There lies a room
Mr Nobody lives there.

I hear him ripping paper,
I hear him scribbling pens,
I hear him sharpening pencils,
He's driving me round the bend!

At the top of the landing
Near the top of the stairs
There lies a room,
Mr Nobody lived there.

I hear no noises,
I think he's moved house.
Wherever he is
He's as quiet as a mouse.

*Sophie Hurst  (10)*
*Davenham CE Primary School*


## UNDER THE SEA

Under the sea
I met a hand fish
And it said to me
I am going this way, that way
Forwards and backwards
Under the red sea.

It met a shark
And his name was Mark
It gobbled him up
And said 'Urrgh it
Tastes like a pup.'

Out he spat the hand fish
And found a coral rock
He bit and
Had an awful shock
His teeth fell out
With a yelping shout!

*Matthew Gilks  (9)*
*Davenham CE Primary School*

## MIST

The sloth crawls slowly along the branch of clouds
Drifting, wondering where to sleep next
Hanging, hanging
Lying over the land
Sleeping, sleeping,
Moving slowly along the cloudy branch.

The sloth slowly moves
Through the jungle of the town
Covering houses in a shapeless cloud
Making rooftops float on its back
Claws feel their way across the dewy ground
It finds a valley to rest for the night
As it sleeps it begins to sleepwalk
Slowly, slowly
Leaving a trail of silver
Seeking, seeking
A new place to sleep
As morning dawns
The sloth fades away
Leaving soft dew on the fresh green grass.

*Kate Trevor & Becky Smith (10)*
*Davenham CE Primary School*


## THE PLUG LADY

The plug lady lives in a bath
Her bubbles make her laugh.

She wanted a cat
But she got a bat.

One day she was eating chips
That day she burnt her lips.

She once bit her tongue
And she smelt an awful pong.

She seemed sad yesterday
How could she be sad in May?

She went and looked at a berry
It surprisingly made her merry!

*Katy Din  (8)*
*Davenham CE Primary School*


## MIST

As gently as the dog's breath
Hovers over the land
He steadily rises over the beach
Brushing over the sand.
Carefully he makes his way
Drifting over treetops
Letting out a fine white dust
Eventually, he reaches the valley
Spreading his magical shower.
The grey-faced dog
Bounds softly into the town
Covering the houses.
His soft, grey feet glide over
The frosty street
The trees' arms frozen with a gentle mist
By morning, the mist
Is a blanket of fine frosty grey.

*Sam Cush, Daniel Williams & James Loveridge  (10)*
*Davenham CE Primary School*

## MIST

The elegant dappled horse,
Waiting for its race,
Prancing on to a different land,
Galloping through towns and villages,
Covering the world in grey smoke
Houses disappear under the mist
Covering grass and flowers,
Watching, waiting,
The eager horse races on,
Mist hangs low over the grass,
Spreading quickly across the river,
Deep into valleys,
Waiting,
The finish line is near,
The race is over,
The mist gently disappears.

*Gina Martin & Angharad Parry  (10)*
*Davenham CE Primary School*


## SEA

The sea is rough,
The sea is tough
For fishermen and sailors
Who cannot get enough
Of the salt and the rain
As they are sailing to Spain
Above the home of the sharks.
It would be my wish
To swim with a school of fish.

*Luke Regan  (7)*
*Davenham CE Primary School*

## MIST

A transparent ghost floating over fields
Covering all that you can see
As though he lies asleep
Making the morning dull and creepy
He swoops over the church steeple sleep
Towards the houses and cottage
Breathing his icy cold breath
Onto the morning air
As dawn approaches
The ghostly grey shadow
Heads over the horizon
The sun rises
On another beautiful day.

*Elizabeth Sutton & Rosie Hilditch (10)*
*Davenham CE Primary School*


## MY FAMILY

My mum plays bingo
Every weekday.
My dad sells cars
At an unfair pay.

My sister makes pancakes
And gets very fat.
My brother has a girlfriend
She's called Pat.

This is my family.

*Katie Hodkinson (9)*
*Davenham CE Primary School*

## LADY ON THE SHIP

The net was hurled up and in sat a mermaid
'Ooh' said the crew as the net was laid
'Ahh' screamed the mermaid 'Get away from me
I'm sure you're going to eat me for your fish tea.'
'No' said the crew still bewitched by the silvery voice
'Well I haven't much choice
I could be dead or
I could rest my head
I will stay as long as I have lots of care.'
They were under her command
Until Captain Blackeye came back I command
But the mermaid was quick and started to sing
'What's your name dear' called Captain Blackeye
Fiddling with a stolen ring.
'Shellsea' she told him
'My middle name's Tim.'
Next day while she slept
The crew with knives to her they crept
'You fools' she cried
As she turned to her side.
She had their golden key
'You' cried her son Lee
And with that he grabbed her tail
And with a great wail
Sent her back to the sea.
'Thanks' said the crew
As they took the key away
And that is the last I will ever say.

*Katie Latta (9)*
*Davenham CE Primary School*

## MIST

Pouncing wolf over the damp fields
Slashing claws attack houses
Tail swishing against bushes
Beady eyes glinting like the moon
Silent as a mouse floating on the soft soil
Wisps past glass windows
Like clouds falling from the sky
As the wolf leaves town
It leaves behind a trail of mist
Into the valley it makes its way
Past icy streams and eerie forests
Floats over rivers
Staring at its silver reflection
In the water
Speeding, sprinting past snowy hills
It creeps into a gloomy cave
Closes its sleepy eyes and settles
Down to sleep
The cloud of mist floats into the town
As the sun comes up
It disappears.

*Amy Bentley & Kenndel Boulton  (10)*
*Davenham CE Primary School*


## ASTERIX AND OBELIX

Asterix has his sword for fights and battles
Obelix scoffs his food up when he's just given it
Mrs Gerryatrix is rude and starts fish fights
Cocophonix is a bard and sings all day and shouts.

*Rowan Southern  (6)*
*Davenham CE Primary School*

## HAVE YOU EVER SEEN SUCH A THING?

Have you ever seen a mermaid on land
Dancing the hula on the sand?
Have you ever seen a pirate on the shore
Hitting and thumping a wild boar?

Have you ever seen a fish
Mumbling and grumbling for a wish?
Have you ever seen a squid
Stuck in a smelly grid?

Have you ever seen such a thing?
Mermaids, pirates, squid and fish
They all make the perfect dish.

*Bethany Foskett (9)*
*Davenham CE Primary School*


## IT'S THE WEEKEND - HOORAY

No alarm clock this morning
Turn over and go back to sleep
There's plenty of time for TV in bed
As it's the weekend - hooray.

No school today, sitting there yawning
Play with my friends, read a good book
A quick game of football
Then back for tea,
As it's the weekend - hooray.

*Sam Kania (9)*
*Davenham CE Primary School*

## THE ENCHANTED SHIP

There's a store of ships near the pier
But there's one you don't know about
The ship it's not really like the name!
But don't tell the pirates
The enchanted ship that's what we call it
It's really called HMS Victory
It's good old Lord Nelson's ship
There's somewhere in London
And that was the name of his last battle.

The Battle of Trafalgar
Where he died aged forty-seven.

*Stephanie Smith (8)*
*Davenham CE Primary School*

## GOING TO THE SEA

Sea, sea everywhere
Sea waving in the air
Making noise like a black mare.

Sea, sea everywhere
See the pirates coming to shore
Get off the ship to see more.

Sea, sea everywhere
See the pirates drinking rum
Then they're saying yum, yum
In my tum, tum, tum.

*Emma Goulbourne (8)*
*Davenham CE Primary School*

## MIST

Untamed ghostly horse
Gallops wildly across fields
Leaving a trail of mist behind.

Hooves skim across the wet dew
Tossing head
White, misty mane covers the mountains.

Swishing tail whips across the grass
Like a deadly snake
Trotting over the hills.

The mist is a silk horse
Floating through the land
Its nostrils twitch in the swooping mist
The sun rises
The gleaming mist disappears.

*Sam Tinker & Lauren (11)*
*Davenham CE Primary School*


## ALONG THE SEA

Along the sea there was a man
He had a fan.

Along the sea there was a mermaid
She was never paid.

Along the sea there was a boat
And the captain was making a note.

Along the sea there was a log
It was in a shape of a frog.

*Hope Maxwell (9)*
*Davenham CE Primary School*

## UNDER THE SEA

Under the sea
There are fishes you see.

Down in the rocks
The mermaids have spots.

On the rusty wrecks
A chicken fish pecks.

But under the sand
There is a hidden land.

And through the green reeds
There are lots of itchy fleas.

But in the treasure chest
There lives a naughty pest!

*Anastasia Dunne  (8)*
*Davenham CE Primary School*


## UNDER THE SEA

Under the sea mermaids swim,
Under the sea fish play games,
Under the sea corals chat,
Under the sea sharks eat fish,
Under the sea lonely shipwrecks lie,
Under the sea people explore,
Under the sea coral reefs protect fish,
Under the sea these things happen,
Under the sea.

*William Galloway  (8)*
*Davenham CE Primary School*

# MIST

Fragile as a butterfly
Fluttering wings
Hover above a milky-white river
Feelers feeling the way on the dew tipped grass
Blurring out the morning view
With its outstretched cloak
Snow-white wings frantically beating
A deep frosty mist
Playing tricks upon your sight
Flying over misty fields
Like someone smoking a pipe
Gently folding wings
The mist settles in the early morning air.

*Amy Sant & Amy Longworth (10)*
*Davenham CE Primary School*


# MIST

A grey, prowling wolf
Creeping through the dewy woods,
Pouncing on damp leaves and tall trees
Stalking the misty town
Breathing on houses,
They disappear in its breath
Pawing gardens
Tail sweeps windows
Hunting its prey,
The clear fields on the horizon.

*Matthew Hall & Liam Nugent (10)*
*Davenham CE Primary School*

## THE MIST

The mist is a white ghost haunting the town
Covering everything with its white, misty trail
Freezing the layer of dew on the hillside
The mist is a white ghost, silent
Trees shouting but only the misty ghost can hear
As they drown under the white sheet.
It flies on over the sea
Sinking ships with its trail
Dissolving oil rigs, the sea turns to snow
The mist is a white ghost, silent
As midday arrives the mist has left without trace
Hibernating, waiting for another night of devastation.

*James & Ben  (10)*
*Davenham CE Primary School*


## THE MIST

Darting, frantic glimmering horse
Hooves skimming over dewy fields
A swishing tail
Leaves a path of mist behind
Ears pricked forwards
Aiming to jump fences and hedges
Galloping, galloping,
Mane flowing
Horseman whipping on cold shoulders
Lean legs leading the way
Cantering, cantering
Covering the fields with a grey misty cloak.

*Rachel Bebbington & Millie Fagan  (11)*
*Davenham CE Primary School*

## MY RABBIT

Found on a driveway, six years ago
A cute, fluffy rabbit as white as the snow
Not finding an owner it needed a home
So I named him Tommy and made him my own.
So off to the pet shop for a hutch and a run
And for hay and some food
All paid for by Mum.
Sometimes he's happy and hops in the sun
Or sometimes he's moody, a real hot cross bun.
He likes carrots and broccoli and juicy green grapes
And dried stuff with seeds in and colourful flakes.
His tickly bobtail and small twitching nose
His pinky, warm ears and soft velvet clothes
So this is the poem of Tommy, my friend
I must go and feed him so the poem must end.

*Josh Hall  (8)*
*Davenham CE Primary School*


## BIRDS

Birds sing in the morning
Just as day is dawning
The birds fly high
Up in the blue sky.

The tree is full of nuts and seed
On which the birds come and feed
They also nest up in the trees
So don't scare them - will you please.

*Becky Coates  (7)*
*Davenham CE Primary School*

## MIST

Steady as the horseman rides
Upon a path of clouds
His grey coat swaying in the breeze
Stirring the dew as he goes
Eyes glowing
Like diamonds in a cave of mist.

A white sheet covering the sky
As his journey comes to an end
On the last leg of his course
The horseman dismounts
As it becomes midday
Steady as the horseman rides
Until a new morning.

*Sarah Capper & Zoë Hancock  (10)*
*Davenham CE Primary School*


## SLIMY SNAKES

Slimy snakes,
Bulging bugs,
Diving ducks,
Flying fudge.
Slivering slugs,
Burping birds,
Dudley dolphins,
Farming flies,
Trying trees,
Bouncing bunnies
Comfy cushions.

*Hannah Parr  (7)*
*Davenham CE Primary School*

# A Cloud Is . . .

A cloud is a sheep in a blue field and it's still roaming on,
A cloud is some candyfloss waiting to be eaten,
A cloud is an angel's cushion,
A cloud is delicious ice cream,
A cloud is some cotton wool.

*Joe Jackson  (8)*
*Davenham CE Primary School*


## Mist

The mist is a haunting ghost
Which blurs the sight of most
Glides over valleys and hills
The misty ghost moves through the town
As the mist leaves its trail of dew
The dew starts to dry
The misty ghost starts to fly.

*Daniel Newton & Thomas Dignum  (10)*
*Davenham CE Primary School*


## Jungle Poem

The monkey is in the trees,
The wind is blowing a breeze,
The birds are singing a song,
The crocodile is humming along.

*Jemma Bently  (8)*
*Davenham CE Primary School*

# BOOKS

Books are great!
They're my best mate.
Short books with eighty pages
Or books that last ages and ages.

Picture books,
Word books,
Books that tell you everything
Even books with music to sing.

Humorous novels or facts from history
Spooky and scary with lots of mystery.
So drift into another world
Exciting adventures as each page unfurls.

*Barry James (11)*
*Forest Park School*


# FIRE

Fire spreading in the night
Giving off gas, giving off light.
Fire running all through the house,
Hissing like a cat after a mouse.
Fire running all around,
Up the wall and across the ground.
It's getting bigger, it's so tall,
It's started running up the wall.
All of a sudden the fire will stop,
And the temperature will drop
With the fire comes the smoke
Dark, acrid, it makes you choke.

*Portia Doré (11)*
*Forest Park School*

## THE RUNNER

Every day on my way to school
I see a man run like a fool,
With two kids running along his side,
People clearing the way far and wide,
Not only does he run and run
It seems he doesn't care about either son.
Why he does this I do not know,
One day I heard his son was absent with a broken toe.
The man's name I think is Tate,
And even if they're early or late,
He keeps on running with his long, lanky pegs
And keeps making the little boys run off their tired, little legs.
He insists on doing this every school day
Which to me is a very big nay, nay,
I know the school is quite far away,
And he should go by car every day.
But then who knows whether Mr Tate
Has a vehicle parked through his gate,
Or he might want to keep the boys fit,
But to me he looks like a complete twit.

*Ashley Houston  (10)*
*Forest Park School*


## BIG BALL OF FIRE

Big ball of fire gleaming skywards
Sticky ice cream fingers
Glinting sandy feet,
Boys skipping school,

Girls gassing in the pool,
Birds singing,
Wind whistling,
Big ball of fire gleaming skywards.

*Sean Flynn  (10)*
*Forest Park School*

## MY COSY CAT

My black cat comes in from the cold
I pick him up to cuddle and hold
His sleek, glossy coat
Is now all flattened and soaked
It is raining hard outside
So Max comes in for somewhere to hide.

My black cat has one thing in mind
A cosy warm place of a welcoming kind
I know just the place
I can tell by his face
We both agree this is the one for me
As ever it will always be.
My lovely, warm, cosy quilt,
Neither of us feel any guilt.
My bed is just so cosy, warm and snug
I give Max a stroke and a little light hug
And say 'Sleep tight and make sure the bugs won't bite.'

*Charlotte Orrell  (10)*
*Forest Park School*

# SCARY POEM

Once upon a time
There was a ghost called Ben
And three little people
Called Mum, Luke and Gwen.
They went for a walk
And met up with ghostly Ben
The ghost said 'We will meet later
In the park near the fox's den.'
Mum said 'Let's have lunch first.'
They had a McDonald's near Big Ben
Then it was time to go
On the way they saw a wren
Singing by the fox's den.
Out popped ghostly Ben
'Hi' said Ben
To Mum, Luke and Gwen
'Please follow me
To my ghostly den.'
They followed Ben
Round the park to his ghostly den
What a surprise they got
For today was ghostly Ben's
Birthday party bash
A birthday cake and candles, ten
And balloons and streamers
Presents from Mum, Luke and Gwen
What a party for ghostly Ben.
Now it was time to sing
'Happy birthday, ghostly Ben
Happy birthday, ten today.'

***Ben Robinson  (8)***
***Gorsey Bank Primary School***

## MY RABBIT BILLY

My rabbit's name is Billy
She's sometimes rather silly
She pushes footballs with her nose
And scratches her ears with her toes.

Her furry ears are very long
And has the cutest little tongue
She pads around on her paws
Often scratches with her claws.

While sitting in her breakfast bowl
And trying to dig a great big hole
She spills her food on the floor
So then we have to give her more.

*Richard Bull  (9)*
*Gorsey Bank Primary School*


## AN AUTUMN MORNING

On the first day of autumn, cold and bitter,
The snow all pattered and pittered.

The path all icy and slippery and wet,
Covered in leaves which were all set.

People all pass, all wrapped up warm,
As the cold, cold air drifts up a storm.

The first leaf drops like a parachute to the floor,
Swifting and swaying in the tree no more.

*Daniel Hassell  (11)*
*Gorsey Bank Primary School*

# ME

I'm really intelligent,
I love to play games,
I have loads of good friends,
I never call names.

So if you want a friend
Why don't you pick me
You might soon be my best friend
Then you'd say whoopee.

My pillow's so soft
Come round for a sleep-over
My bed's really comfy
I never say move over.

That's me!

*Emily Perrett (7)*
*Gorsey Bank Primary School*


# THE ELEPHANT'S CHILD

I saw the elephant storming across the plains
Her big feet stamping in the dusty dirt
Her calf wandering beside her.
Her grey skin looks tired against the heated sun
Bang! Goes the gun
Down goes the elephant
Her last breath for her calf
Her child.

*Jessica Riley (10)*
*Gorsey Bank Primary School*

# THE SUN

When the sun comes I smile
It makes our lives seem worthwhile.
I like playing in the blazing sun
Every day is very fun.
Having a picnic in the park
And playing on the big ark
They always remind me
Of happy days in the sun.

*Danielle Harrison (9)*
*Gorsey Bank Primary School*


# DELAMERE FOREST

Trees that grow as tall as buildings,
Life and death is in the air.
Moss that feels as soft as fur,
Birds that sing as sweet as choirs.
Wild berries that taste of wine,
Let this forest be forever.

*Beth Morris (9)*
*Gorsey Bank Primary School*


# WOODS

In the woods it's dark and scary
It makes you shiver like a fairy.
In the woods it's cold and wet
Make sure you wrap up
You don't want a cold, you don't want the flu
So put your coat on and zip it up tight!

*Abigail MacPherson (8)*
*Gorsey Bank Primary School*

## THE WOODS

Silent air, hear the birds tweeting
Textured trees covering the sky
Thin ones, fat ones, even stumps left in the ground
Pebbles and stones hiccuping the ground.
Long, thin, slender branches that is the tree
We call the silver birch
Orange and green leaves
Making a lush carpet.

*Zoe Perera  (9)*
*Gorsey Bank Primary School*

## SPIDERS

Spiders are creepy
You better watch out.
They can creep on your bed
You better watch out.
They can go anywhere, anywhere at all
You better, better, better, better,
Better watch out.

*Charlotte Ricketts*
*Gorsey Bank Primary School*

## HIDDEN TREASURES

Blue sky without a cloud in sight,
Warm sun on my face,
Soft sand under my feet,
Cool waves splashing over them,
This is perfect.
Posh boats are in the peaceful harbour,
People are relaxing and watching the world go by,
Slipping into the pool to cool off,
After a hot day in Spain,
Happy memories,
Hidden treasures.

*Laura White (10)*
*Hartford Primary School*


## MY HIDDEN TREASURE

My hidden treasure is my future
Hidden from me
None can see, none can know
My hidden treasure
Hidden deep in me.

My hidden treasure may be my children
And my future family.
My future is my hidden treasure,
Hidden deep in me.

*Max Ling (10)*
*Hartford Primary School*

## ONCE A LITTLE GIRL

Once I was a little girl
Happy and cheery and bright
I wish I was still a little girl
Just starting to read and write.

But now I'm all grown up you see
I can't get away with things
I wish I was still only three
I'm thinking this when the doorbell rings.

Mum says 'Come in' then the door slams shut
I hear 'Thank you. You're welcome.'
And they stroke the cat called Soot.

Smash, bang, trollop
There goes mum's vase
Dad gives Soot a wallop
And my mum looks like she's flown to Mars.

Mum's having an eppy
While Dad's drinking beer
I ask for my Double Decky
And I get a clip round the ear.

I start to cry
And everybody stares
But now I'm that bit older
Nobody cares.

*Lydia Whitley  (10)*
*Hartford Primary School*

# THE MAGIC HUT

I will put in the Hitler hut . . .

His evil grin as he towers over the Jews,
The happiness of the British after he surrenders,
The terror of his victims before he killed them.

I will put in The Blitz hut . . .

The petrified look of the survivors of The Blitz,
The cold feeling of the air around the site of the bombing,
The terrified scream of a small child buried in the rubble.

I will put in the Blackout hut . . .

The haunting deep black vision of the dark streets,
The sounds of the dreaded German Luftwaffe,
The agonising thought of death as the buzzing noise drifts above.

I will put in the World War One hut . . .

The sad memories of the perished soldiers,
The devastating effect of the gas sent by the Germans,
The deafening noise of the murderous fighters.

*Tom Connolly  (10)*
*Lacey Green Primary School*


# THE MOON

Curled up baby inside a mother's womb,
A blood vein taking and giving food,
A sleeping eye, dozing through day.
Napping through night,
Like Sleeping Beauty, waiting for light.

*Abigail Walker  (8)*
*Lacey Green Primary School*

## A CHILD'S WAR

I'm only a little child
Who needs to go to bed
But the planes are flying low tonight
And the bombs blow up in my head.

I'm only a little child
I'm very nearly nine
And the enemy in the sky tonight
His blood's the same as mine.

I'm only a little child
And the noises are too loud
Screaming through my nightmares
In a blackened smoke-filled cloud.

I'm only a little child,
I'm scared of things that fly
And I don't know the enemy
And I don't want to die.

*Corin Belyeu (10)*
*Lacey Green Primary School*


## SIMILES

As slow as a lamb, as cunning as a giant
As wise as a kitten, as white as a mouse,
As quiet as a bee, as blind as a fox.

As busy as a ghost, as heavy as a bat,
As tall as an owl, as playful as an elephant.

*Paul Brereton (11)*
*Lacey Green Primary School*

## WAR

When I know the enemies are in the sky
I feel a tear come to the corner of my eye.
I get this feeling, sort of a sensation
I know sooner or later I'll get moved to a different destination.

When you hear a bomb you get glued to the spot,
I've heard of these camps - apparently you get shot,
I can't help getting this feeling that I'm going to die.
I hope one day up there, they'll be our allies.
I'm only a child, believe me it's true,
We're all the same, them . . . me and you.

*Olivia Lamon (11)*
*Lacey Green Primary School*


## THE MOON

The moon is like a golden snitch, hovering in the air,
A floating, speeding bludger, taking its morning dare,
A levitating quaffle, as light as a strand of hair.

The moon is like a silver rainbow, glazing in the sky,
A dilapidated, spinning globe, a watchful golden eye,
A shining mysterious glow, sparkling up on high.

The moon is like a fingernail, curved and reflecting light,
An orange slice of mango, taken by a bite
A half moon shining clearly, peeping through the night.

*Shannan Sutton (9)*
*Lacey Green Primary School*

## TOM

Tom is . . .

A roaring lion
Crawling through the jungle.

The tip of a pencil
Balancing on a rooftop.

As angry as a teacher,
Shouting at a child.

A sharp nail
Scratching on a window.

As loud as a giant,
Crushing a tower.

He is as dark as a deep, deep hole.

Like a bomb launching from a cannon.

But he never gets to do the thing that he wants.

*Lewis Millar  (10)*
*Lacey Green Primary School*


## NEW HOUSE

My steps echo through the hall,
The window ledge is dusty,
The garage door needs paint,
The handle is all rusty!

The kitchen walls have dirty marks,
Bedroom walls have too,
The bathroom door is missing,
There's a lot of work to do!

*Fiona Varney (11)*
*Lacey Green Primary School*

## WHAT IS THE SUN?

The sun is a yellow sunflower,
Waving goodbye to the wet rain.

It is a yellow light bulb,
Being ordered to work.

It is an orange ball,
Rolling on the cold, hard, dark table.

It is a yellow clock ticking away
Passing time in the old, lonely room.

It is an orange plate
On a black surface.

An orange beach ball
Heading to Heaven.

*Hollie Gray (9)*
*Lacey Green Primary School*

## THERE'S A BUMP

There's a bump, there's a bump,
There's a bump, in the middle of the road.

There's a car on the bump,
In the middle of the road.

There's a bump, there's a bump,
There's a bump, in the middle of the road.

There's a car with a cat on a bump,
In the middle of the road.

There's a bump, there's a bump,
There's a bump, in the middle of the road.

There's a car with a cat and a spider,
On the bump in the middle of the road.

There's a bump, there's a bump,
There's a bump, in the middle of the road.

There's a car with a cat and a spider and a bat,
On the bump in the middle of the road.

There's a bump, there's a bump,
There's a bump, in the middle of the road.

There's a car with a cat with a spider and a bat and a flea
There's a bump, in the middle of the road.

There's a bump, there's a bump,
There's a bump, in the middle of the road

*Jordan McAlees  (9)*
*Lacey Green Primary School*

## MY LIFE

Is . . .

As busy as a bee,
As a bumblebee.

As cute as a lamb,
As a golden, white lamb.

As black as a spider,
As a creeping spider.

As settled as a cat,
As a sleeping cat in the sun.

That's my life!

*Elizabeth Wilson (10)*
*Lacey Green Primary School*


## ANIMALS

As playful as a kitten,
As busy as a bee,
As slow as a snail,
As wise as an owl,
As quiet as a fox,
As gentle as a lamb,
As tall as an elephant,
As cunning as a ghost,
As white as a mouse,
As blind as a bat,
As heavy as a giant.

*Jessica Toombs (9)*
*Lacey Green Primary School*

## MY NAN

I have a nan that lives far away,
I long for that day that she comes to stay,
She's as soft as a dolly,
Cheerful and jolly,
She's as bright as a spark,
And sings like a lark,
She is getting old,
But she's still as bold,
I'll be sad when it's her time to leave,
I'll wail and weep into my sleeve,
But then I'll remember the memories I keep,
And no longer feel the need to weep.

*Aaron Murphy  (10)*
*Lacey Green Primary School*


## THE MANHATTAN GRAVEYARD

Why did this happen? How can this be?
No one could stop them, you nor me.
The two twin towers fell to the ground,
In ten seconds flat with a rumbling sound.
They took years to build, to fall in a second,
To the Afghans victory beckoned.
Tuesday the eleventh of September,
Will be a day, all Americans remember
Ten thousand dead, twenty-five thousand hurt,
Fifteen thousand buried in rubble and dirt.

*Stephanie Bowyer  (10)*
*Moulton Primary School*

## THE DOG AND THE FROG

There once was a dog called Gigglegog
Whose best friend was a little green frog.

They went on strange adventures together
Even if it was rainy weather.

The frog and the dog went to hunt
But they found their long swords were blunt.

They carried on through the wood
But frog found himself sinking in mud.

Gigglegog tried to pull out the frog,
'I can't help you,' cried the scared dog.

Then frog found himself in bed
With a bandage around his sore head.

Little frog had only one friend,
But Gigglegog said 'It will last till the end.'

*Samantha Walsh  (10)*
*Moulton Primary School*


## THE TALLEST TREE

In the black, thick forest I always search around
One day in my biggest adventure I found the tallest tree
All the rest are small and thin but this is the king of all the trees
I climb to the top and look at the whole world
I can see my house and my friend's house
I've been to the tallest tree.

*Emily Lindsay  (10)*
*Moulton Primary School*

## BARMY DAD

My dad,
Barmy as ever
Falls out of bed day and night
And so he joined the Army.

But

They thought he was barmy.

Mum,
Lent him her best boots
Which he left on the conveyor belt
At work
And it got turned into
Salami.

When Mum found out
She went

*Scatty, batty,*

And blew up his bed with
Dynamite!

After that
She blew up his car with
*A rail gun!*

Then

She joined the Army
*And she blew Barmy Dad up with*
*A bazooka!*
And got shot herself by
An exploding sheep!

And so that was the end
Of the Barmy family
Who got killed
In the Army.

*Steven Knowles  (10)*
*Moulton Primary School*


## SNOWFLAKE

Silvery patterns,
Glisten in the sun.
Melting away,
Reminds me of life.
Full of coldness,
Just one in a crowd,
Everyone is different,
Being trampled into the ground,
Or blown about by the wind,
But in a way they're all the same,
They fall crisp and new,
Join on the way down,
Make each other stronger,
Then crash to the ground,
Become weak,
And melt away,
Like life.

*Lara Pointon  (11)*
*Moulton Primary School*

## MY FRIEND STEPH

My friend Steph likes boys!
T
A
L
L
Boys
Small boys
Thick boys,
Blond boys,
Dark boys,
Strong boys,
Fat boys,
Thin boys,
Mean boys,
Kind boys,
My friend Steph likes boys!
Any kind of boys!

My friend Steph likes make-up
Blue make-up,
Cool make-up,
Pink make-up,
Green make-up,
Bright make-up,
Pale make-up,
Silver make-up,
Gold make-up,
Red make-up,
Yellow make-up,
Orange make-up,
Black make-up,

My friend Steph likes make-up!
Any kind of make-up.

But most of all my friend Steph
Likes me!

*Emma Heath (11)*
*Moulton Primary School*


## MY BROTHER

My brother is cool,
My brother is sad.
My brother is lazy,
Just like my dad.
He plays on the PlayStation,
All the time with me,
But one week he didn't
Because he had his BCG.

He supports Liverpool,
It's all over his wall.
I only walk in,
And he kicks me with a ball.

That's my brother
He plays on the wreck.
And now you can tell,
He's a pain in the neck!

*Kurt Davies (11)*
*Moulton Primary School*

## THE WEIRD FAMILY

I had an Uncle Fred
He couldn't get out of bed
Because he's my uncle Fred.

I had a Grandma Jane
Who even forgot her name
Because she's my Grandma Jane.

I had an Uncle Dill
Who forgot to take his pill
He told Uncle Fred
And ended up dead
Because he's my uncle Dill.

I had a dad called Danny
Who turned into a granny
A weird dad I had.

I had an Uncle Mike
Who caught a ten foot pike
That's my pike meaning Mike.

I had a fish called Trevor
Who wasn't very clever
He swims through his tank
Like a submarine that sank.

I had a friend called Jack
Who gave his brother a smack
Then he hit Jack back
Jack's a good friend to have.

I have a weird family and friends
We are a happy lot
We are like peas in a pot.

*Stephen McNichol  (10)*
*Moulton Primary School*

## MY MUM

My mum is kind and loving
She always buys me sweets
She is always joyful
To everyone she meets.

My mum is full of laughter
She makes me feel so bright
My mum she gives me confidence
Every day and night.

My mum does all the cleaning
She always asks us why.
She also does the cooking
Especially cottage pie.

My mum is the best
She is not like all the rest.
My mum is the best in town
Yes, yes, yes!

*Katie Casselden (10)*
*Moulton Primary School*


## POEMS

Poems are good, poems are bad,
You can choose of what poems you want
Poems are funny, poems are sad,
Maybe a tissue or a good laugh you will have
Poems are precious, poems are worthless,
Just keep one in mind and you'll get along fine
So whatever the poem, it's a type of poem,
Remember this poem, when you read your own poem.

*Thomas Boardman (11)*
*Moulton Primary School*

## CATTLEFIELD, BATTLEFIELD

We went into a cattlefield
To try and find some cows
Alas, alak we then found out
That it had been a battlefield.

We found a giant crater
At the foot of a large pine
And at the bottom, surprise, surprise
An unexploded mine.

We fell into the crater
With a resounding clang
And afterwards the villagers heard
A loud and horrible bang.

*David Milnes  (10)*
*Moulton Primary School*


## AUNTY LIZ

My aunty Liz is the best, she cooks and cleans day and night
She loves seeing fireworks and loves the *bang!*
And also loves crackers which also go *bang!*
She has a cat
That sits on her mat
She loves seeing me which she loves most
She loves seeing me with her pussy cat
That sits on her mat
She has a husband called Mike
And he has a motorbike.
Lives in a cottage and I don't know where,
I think it is the middle of nowhere.

*Francesca Pryce  (10)*
*Moulton Primary School*

## WINTER

Crystal feathers flutter to the ground
Glittery grams of snow slowly melting
Blankets of snow, tucking the garden to sleep
Trees like black-suited soldiers keep guard
Falling icicles like silver spikes, trapping you
Flickering flames with golden, orange glow
A cosy, warm welcome waves to you
A clatter of hooves on the roof
A loud pair of feet
A scraping sound in the chimney
Santa pops out!
Christmas is here!

*Justin Lewis (11)*
*Murdishaw West Community Primary School*


## FROSTY WINTER

Freezing cold snow in the winter's wind
Snowflakes dancing down from the sky
Flakes silently twirling through the clouds
Like floating feathers landing on the ground
A giant's pillow covering the garden
A thick, white blanket touching the ground
Footprints crunching in the snow
A soldier snowman watching over the plants
Standing like a statue in the garden.

*Ryan Stevenson (9)*
*Murdishaw West Community Primary School*

## PERSEUS

P erseus' mother was cradling Perseus in her arms while the water was
crashing against it.
E ager to escape from the roar of the waves in that battered chest
R efusing not to give up with Perseus in her arms
S uddenly they heard a thud, to their amazement there was a man
standing over them
E agerly powerful Perseus plunged his sword into Medusa.
U sing his helmet he got to kill the horrible Medusa
S pitting, hissing snakes of Medusa's head died too, but her eyes were
still open so if anything looked into them they would turn to stone.

*Zak Chaudri (9)*
*Murdishaw West Community Primary School*


## PERSEUS

P oor Andromeda was chained to the sharp, cold rocks on the sandy
hot beach
E vil King Acrisius locked beautiful, kind Princess Danane away in a
tall tower
R aging Acrisius found out that his beautiful, kind Danane had a child
S hield given to him from the powerful god Athena
E verybody waiting for Perseus to return with the head of the
horrid Medusa
U nseen Perseus chopped off Medusa's head
S atisfied, Perseus completed his challenge.

*Laura Graham (10)*
*Murdishaw West Community Primary School*

## PERSEUS

P erseus' mother was protecting him in her arms inside the chest,
E agerly trying to escape from the waves that were battering the
wooden drawer,
R efusing not to give up,
S uddenly they felt a bump on the shore and the chest opened and a
fisherman appeared,
E very day they lived happily on Seriphos
U ntil they were invited to a feast and told to bring gifts,
S orry was the boasting Perseus.

*Sam Dougan (10)*
*Murdishaw West Community Primary School*


## PERSEUS, THE PURE-HEARTED HERO

P ure-hearted Perseus plunges his sword towards the evil Medusa
E vil screeches come from the gorgon sisters
R aging waves where he finds Andromeda
S ea creature comes out of the ocean and our brave hero turns
it to stone
E very step he takes he moves closer to his mother
U gly Medusa's head turns the people of the court to stone
S oon after Perseus killed his grandfather the King Acrisius.

*Imogen Maxwell (10)*
*Murdishaw West Community Primary School*

## THE SUMMER WIND

The summer wind
Is lovely and kind
It comes so gently
And then goes behind
The garden shed.
The summer wind is loving and soft.
I love the summer
It's the best ever.

*Daniel Brown  (9)*
*Murdishaw West Community Primary School*

## THE WINTER WIND

The winter wind is strong,
It whistles a little song.
It's so rough,
It can blow stuff.
A stick,
Or even a brick.
The wind spins,
I like the wind.

*Gemma Vidamour  (9)*
*Murdishaw West Community Primary School*

## MY SUMMER WIND

The summer wind is such a breeze
It hits right upon my knees.
It's so kind, so gentle
You know it drives me mental
It's the summer wind.

*Aaron Astles  (9)*
*Murdishaw West Community Primary School*

## SUMMER WIND

The summer wind
Is gentle and kind
It's loving and generous all the time.
All my family like the summer wind
Because it is the best.
The sun goes behind the garden shed
Then he goes straight to bed.

*Leanne Moore  (9)*
*Murdishaw West Community Primary School*


## THE SUMMER WIND

The summer wind
Is kind and gentle
Tanned by the sun
Keeps me cool on the hottest day
It softly sweeps along
It is like a hairdryer outside.

*Chloe Jones  (8)*
*Murdishaw West Community Primary School*


## THE AUTUMN WIND

The autumn wind is naughty
It blows the leaves off the trees.
The autumn breeze is so crafty and mischievous
And guides the rubbish down the street.
The autumn gale swifts your washing.

*Daniel Hughes  (8)*
*Murdishaw West Community Primary School*

## THE SUMMER WIND

The summer wind
Is kind and sweet
It makes my hair
Nice and hot.
It reminds me of holidays
And it is a sweet wind.

*Kelly Grundy (9)*
*Murdishaw West Community Primary School*

## THE WINTER WIND

The winter wind is tough and nobody can escape
The wind is evil and is like a tornado.
A tornado sucks you up and never lets you down.
The wind can knock you into a fence
If you are underground the wind can't get you.

*Liam Sanders (8)*
*Murdishaw West Community Primary School*

## THE SUMMER WIND

The summer wind is soft and gentle
And the wind is loving.
It blows softly and lovely
Soft as a sweet
The wind will come back.

*Sallyann Gobin (9)*
*Murdishaw West Community Primary School*

## PERSEUS

P owerful Perseus crept to Medusa
E erie scream from the evil gorgons
R attling snakes inside the bag, hissing and spitting
S erpent from Medusa's head, hissing like never before
E cho scream in the air, everyone starts to stare
U nknown what was in the bag until they were turned to stone
S illy King Acrusius, dead as a doornail.

*Abbie-Gayle Haskayne (10)*
*Murdishaw West Community Primary School*

## GORGONS

G reat serpents stretching slowly and spitting
O dd twisting statues all around
R apid rage floods through Perseus as he draws his sword
G entle Pegasus flows from the corpse
O verflowing serpents curl up rapidly
N ature regains itself as the blood of Medusa drips on the ground
S andals with wings take him on his journey.

*Laura Voss (10)*
*Murdishaw West Community Primary School*

## GORGONS

G orgon Medusa eagerly seeking the next to be stone
O bserving from the shield the powerful Medusa
R apidly hissing and spitting from Medusa's serpent hair
G lancing into her eyes would turn you to stone
O ptions won't work
N amed but not shamed is mighty Perseus
S triking first is Perseus.

*Robert Grainger (10)*
*Murdishaw West Community Primary School*

# A TASTE OF AUTUMN

Taste autumn in the woods
In the golden trees
In the twirling leaves.

Taste it in the fingers of spooky mist
In bright firework colours
In the smoky bonfires.

Taste autumn in sweet apples
In juicy pears
In my garden.

*Amanda Orme  (9)*
*Murdishaw West Community Primary School*


# PERSEUS, PROUD OF HIS POWER

P   roud of his mother for protecting him.
E   xecuted Medusa because of her sin
R   evenge he claimed on King Acrisius for throwing him and his
                                        mother into the ocean.
S   acrificed Andromeda to the slippery serpent of the sea
E   veryone waiting impatiently to see if Perseus succeeds
U   ltra-violent battles Perseus called
S   atisfied with winning his challenge.

*Chelsea Morgan  (9)*
*Murdishaw West Community Primary School*

## PERSEUS, THE ULTIMATE WARRIOR

P owerful Perseus plunging his sword into Medusa
E agerly Perseus waiting to chop off Medusa's head
R aging the discus into the sky hitting an old man on the head
S howing the head of Medusa turning everyone to stone
E ach step taken by Perseus moved him closer to Medusa
U ltimate Perseus killing Medusa and using the head to stop
the sea monster
S hield that Athena gave Perseus helps Perseus kill Medusa.

*Nathan Southern (9)*
*Murdishaw West Community Primary School*


## PERSEUS

P oor Perseus wondering how to kill Medusa
E ager to free Danae from King Polydectes
R age heats his blood as he kills Medusa
S creams from the gorgons fill the air
E vil Medusa was dead at long last
U nder the protection of Zeus he returns home
S oon Perseus marries Andromeda and lives happily with his family.

*Charlotte McCormick (10)*
*Murdishaw West Community Primary School*


## THE SUMMER WIND

The summer wind is kind and gentle
It makes my hair nice and hot
It is very loving for me to play in.
The summer wind is generous
It keeps us clean all the time.

*Nikki Williams (9)*
*Murdishaw West Community Primary School*

## PERSEUS AND THE GORGONS

P owerful Perseus carries the head of Medusa
E erie screams from the three horrible gorgons
R oyal King Polydectes waits for the head of Medusa
S pecial gifts from the gods, goddesses and nymphs
E veryone waiting impatiently for Perseus
U sing his winged sandals Perseus flies to the gorgon's home
S aving his mother Perseus felt glad.

*Chelsea Davies  (10)*
*Murdishaw West Community Primary School*


## THE SUMMER WIND

The summer wind so soft and sweet,
It brings the breeze to my feet
It reminds me of my holiday in Spain,
When I went on the plane.
My mum puts the fan on because she's hot,
She says she feels like hot pot.
The summer wind is the best,
Not like winter wind, it's a pest.

*Amy Brown  (9)*
*Murdishaw West Community Primary School*


## SUMMER WIND

The summer wind reminds me of a person
She is kind, loving, caring
She makes my hair go fuzzy
She makes me go all funny.
The summer wind makes me invent a game
Then it's time to go.

*Wade Johnston  (8)*
*Murdishaw West Community Primary School*

## PERSEUS

P owerful Perseus plunging his sword into Medusa
E agerly Perseus waits to chop off Medusa's head.
R aging, his sword killing Medusa
S hield of Athena helps Perseus to see and kill Medusa
E ach step took him closer to the gorgons
U ltimate Perseus killing Medusa and using the head to kill monsters.
S howing the head of Medusa and turning everyone to stone.

*Joel Yates (9)*
*Murdishaw West Community Primary School*

## POWERFUL PERSEUS

P owerful Perseus takes the plunge
E agerly he swings his sword
R usty and bloodstained he wipes his sword along the grass
S ilvering serpents screaming on her head
E vil gorgon sisters look around for their enemy
U gly gorgons hear Medusa scream
S creaming Medusa is now dead.

*Sophie Spencer-Duggan (9)*
*Murdishaw West Community Primary School*

## GORGONS

G reen gruesome gorgons sleeping silently
O utstanding overgrown serpents slithering everywhere
R ocky statues that were once people
G argoyle statues hanging off the wall
O verjoyed Perseus raises his sword
N oisy Medusa screams as she is decapitated
S aving Andromeda from the dreaded sea monster.

*Kate Healey (10)*
*Murdishaw West Community Primary School*

## GORGONS

G  orgons protecting Medusa
O  ne of the gorgons starts to attack
R  aging out of the sea comes a monster
G  liding in the sky comes Perseus with flying sandals
O  ver Medusa's head wakes a snake
N  ight-time comes while Perseus arrives
S  tretching widely out comes Perseus creeping forward to Medusa.

*Kerry Horabin  (10)*
*Murdishaw West Community Primary School*


## PERSEUS, THE HERO

P  erseus out for the head of Medusa
E  normous snakes tangled together
R  aging eyes staring at Perseus
S  tatues stand where people stood
E  nemy Medusa shrivelled and died
U  nder risk he strikes his sword
S  andals help him on his quest.

*Anthony Moore  (10)*
*Murdishaw West Community Primary School*


## PERSEUS, THE WINGED WARRIOR

P  owerful Perseus forced his sword from Hermes into Medusa
E  ager to get back to King Acricius
R  attling snakes are in Medusa's hair
S  tabbing Medusa you can hear an eerie scream
E  verlasting snakes are still spitting and hissing
U  nder the invisibility helmet Perseus creeps past the three grey sisters
S  till sounds of the snakes in Medusa's hair.

*Elisha Storrow  (9)*
*Murdishaw West Community Primary School*

## THE WINTER WIND IS STRONG

The winter wind is strong
And it blows people along
It's rough and tough
And never gives up
And a storm can
Mess up a lawn.
Some people are unkind
So is the winter wind.
The winter wind is
The strongest of them all.

*Andrew Kelley (9)*
*Murdishaw West Community Primary School*

## PERSEUS, THE WINGED WARRIOR

P    oor Danae plunged into the sea with her young baby Perseus
E    vil Medusa opened one eye
R    oyal King Acrisius challenged Perseus to kill Medusa
S    creaming was heard from the cruel gorgons
E    erie Perseus chopped off Medusa's head to show the king
U    nder the clouds with his winged sandals
S    atisfied Perseus completed his task.

*Zoe Pullan (9)*
*Murdishaw West Community Primary School*

## THE SUMMER WIND IS KIND

The summer wind is kind
It is generous at all times
When it is warm
It blows softly at you
It relaxes your lovely body
You feel loved
At all sweetly times
And the breeze is gentle.

*Natalie Lloyd  (9)*
*Murdishaw West Community Primary School*

## THE SUMMER WIND

The summer wind
Is sweet and generous
It makes my hair nice and hot
It makes you think of the birds that fly
And that butterflies flutter in the sky.
It sweeps the leaves off the ground
It's a sweetly sound.

*Laura Bentley  (8)*
*Murdishaw West Community Primary School*

# HIDDEN TREASURE

A sunken galleon coloured like a volcano there lies in the
ocean bed nearby.
There lieth a chrome goblet a piece of golden ingot encrusted with
jewels at the bottom of the sealed chest.
Upon the sandy ocean bed embedded in the seaweed, a rusty chest
resteth like a fungi-covered rock.
Behind the towering wreck a carpet of garnets like a flower bed
of roses there lieth.
Upon the rotten deck they findeth a gilded carpet of coins like
a sheet of gold.
There hideth 'neath the stern of the ship a row of kegs full to the brim
with the captain's rum reserves.
Below the surface above the seabed a mast like a derelict drainpipe
there hangeth.
In the shadow of the rocks a decaying wooden hull there standeth.
On the bow of the wreck watchful of the surrounding standeth
carved mermaid.

*Rebecca Perkins (10)*
*St Mary's CE Primary School, Sale*


# HIDDEN TREASURES

A history filled book on the bottom of the ocean there lies,
Like a new crowned King a goblet standeth feels proud and tall,
Like a shy little child, a rusty old chest hideth, half buried in the sand,
Brass is the ship's wheel, which also is a turned cog,
Figurehead they ship's look-out, constantly stareth ahead which
walketh on the tip of the waves,
Jewels and gems on the cockle seaweed bed in infinite piles shine.

*Ella Billson (10)*
*St Mary's CE Primary School, Sale*

## HIDDEN TREASURES

In front of my observing eyes there standeth a disused goblet
                                        like a proud sailor.
A rusty chest upon the ocean there lies like a forlorn, abandoned
                                        package.
Like a forgotten carriage wheel, the ship's wheel doth sit,
embedded in the soft, grainy sand.
Jewels and coins interspersed between thy bones and bodies like
twinkling stars woven in the midnight sky.
A mocking wooden mermaid, thy figurehead woos the doubtful
sea creatures to make her their habitat.
Glistening coins, dispersed by the angry current art scattered by.
Drunkenly, like jolly sailors upon the deck, battered kegs of run do lie.
Bedecked with barnacles, the ancient mast, like a giant's spine
doth emerge from thy mysterious, watery world.

*Sarah Donovan  (10)*
*St Mary's CE Primary School, Sale*


## HIDDEN TREASURES

There upon the seabed still there lies a goblet rotting, pampered
                                        by jewels.
Nay an abandoned chest like orphan awaits to reveal his true secrets
                                        locked inside.
There lies upon the seaweed bed a mast half torn like a rag doll worn.
Thy jewels are summoned in kegs of rum awaiting a sentence buried
                                        or torn.
Coins that sunk centuries ago embedded in thy strangling seaweed
                                        strong.
Thy chipped figurehead protecting thy shuddering shipwreck,
forever guarding secrets locked inside.

*Siân Whitefoot  (10)*
*St Mary's CE Primary School, Sale*

## HIDDEN TREASURES

Far below upon the deep there lies a wealthy galleon with a figure head,
the face of a queen that there did sit upon the waves.
I then there saw a rusty historic chest covered in sand like an unwanted,
crumbly biscuit.
On the sandy bed, jewels rest like scattered shiny stones next to stale
spilling rum that was once drunk by man.
I now there see thy ship's brass wheel that lies beyond the extensive
mast like a spiral balancing upon a stick.
A goblet sprawls embedded in damp sand like an abandoned pop-out
artwork covered in dust-like sand beside the enormous hull that there
rests in peace.
Why look, it's the metal cannon that there did fiercely fire at stranger
ships that there did trespass on the galleon's waters.

*Sally Jowett (10)*
*St Mary's CE Primary School, Sale*


## HIDDEN TREASURES

The ancient, rusty galleon like an erupting volcano there shivers.
A decaying goblet lies like an abandoned statue to be discovered
waiting.
A tarnished chest yonder the manlike sea urchin lieth.
The vessel's brass wheel still moveth as though someone still remains.
Inside an old food box forgotten coins resteth like they are in a deep
sleep.
Silver jewels like the orange star shineth.
Kegs of rum smell like a drunken sailor roteth.
The mast still proudly like ye owl standeth.
A golden mermaid for a young man searcheth.

*Katherine Deverell-Smith (11)*
*St Mary's CE Primary School, Sale*

## HIDDEN TREASURES

Upon a strong table there before my scanning eyes,
a brave golden goblet stands there for thy world to see
like a knight of a kingly warrior ship from a bloody battle returning.

Beneath the flowing sea a treasure chest lies in the strangling sea
grass hiding.
Inside thy yellow treasure chest diamonds plus gems for years gone by
lies simmering silently thy gems and diamonds shine bright like lights
in a dark room fading.

Upon a ship deck stands a proud wheel brass, when thy victorious
captain should turn the fine wheel as though it was a grandfather
clock's hands being turned round or a horse drawn carriage's wheel
turning round as the horse tows it along.
As it navigates when to go the unbearable heat of the kingly sun beats
down on him like a drummer beating a drum.

*Lucy Longmore  (11)*
*St Mary's CE Primary School, Sale*


## HIDDEN TREASURES

A rusty chest that there layeth upon the sandy bed like a log
embedded there in soft soil.
The glistening brass plated wheel there rests upon the hull that there
had lain nearby.
A goblet that there was concealed inside the eye of the golden
figurehead like a sad old keg that inside the hull of the galleon perched.
Thousands of jewels that were scattered lay upon the sandy bed
like stars and planets there glinting in every snicket and corner of the
illuminated midnight sky.

*Robert Hardwick  (11)*
*St Mary's CE Primary School, Sale*

## HIDDEN TREASURES

I saw a thousand schools of fish and wrecks upon the billowing waves,
frightfully so.
A golden goblet upon the ocean floor,
Skulls and skeletons with ruby and crystal eyes in holes of skulls
nearby, staring back.
A figurehead carved so carefully covered with barnacles that are like
cobwebs and spiders upon cover the body of the beautiful mermaid,
smiling.
An ancient chest with brass bars is half buried in sand crumbling
before my very eyes.
I seeth a keg flooding the area with its last drops of rum.
Upon the ship carries many secrets.
Old coins rusting upon the deck falling away pearls shine brightly in
a darkened corner, beckoning me to come near.
More skeletons lie around giving homes to fish and crabs, on the
bones gnawing.
A man's skeleton still has on his boots and a shredded shirt that is
trying to clutch anything upon the deck that passes.

*Emily Mann (10)*
*St Mary's CE Primary School, Sale*


## HIDDEN TREASURES

A rusty chest there lies upon the deserted ocean bed
like a dormouse the silent predator is watching.
The ship's wheel there lies upon the galleon
nigh the rusty old chest holding secrets.
I seeth scattered by goblets like cups there lying congested
with jewels.
The mast standeth proud of the watery tomb
protector of the bounty of the kegs of rum hideth in the murky
depth of the hull.

*Helen Robinson (10)*
*St Mary's CE Primary School, Sale*

## HIDDEN TREASURES

I saw a glistening goblet, which shone upon a vast galleon
like a coin upon a deserted house.
A rusty chest there lies on a sandy ocean bed like a sleeping dog.
Ripped and torn the ancient ingot standeth as if it has been let down
by the keen worker ants that once crept below it.
Standing proud and tall like the Statue of Liberty,
there is a figurehead for once it there stood on the prow of a great
and powerful ship.
Whining in the midnight sky, rusty old coins infest priceless and
glinting jewels that shine like the moon on a dark night.
In the centre of the galleon cries a lonely wheel as so does a fish
being eaten by a shark, its rusty handles can barely move.

*Harry Raphael  (10)*
*St Mary's CE Primary School, Sale*


## HIDDEN TREASURES

Lain on the bottom of the deep, thou forgotten goblets shimmery
like the brightest star.
The ill-gotten rusty chest drifteth down to thy mocking fathoms
under the frothing water.
Oh brass plated wheel embedded in the shifting sand,
a piece of wrap stuck in a clasping rock.
Glinting jewels stare lifelessly into space like unblinking eyes.
Angry coins clatter down the perilous rocks.
Empty, soulless kegs drift down to meet the ocean bed.
Thy proud mast out of the wreck like a giant's spear protrudes.
The kingly figurehead is mocked by the gruesome seaweed
and the great hull rests like a giant animal slumbering.

*Thomas Biddulph  (10)*
*St Mary's CE Primary School, Sale*

## HIDDEN TREASURES

A rusty goblet lieth shivering like an abandoned egg cup alone.
An antique chest on the soft gritty bed of sand sits like a
jewellery box upon a dressing table.
A ship's wheel creaks upon a pile of stones like an old broken door,
forgotten.
I see a bag of coins swaying in the murky sea like a flag in the wind
floating.
Kegs of rum stand like proudeth kings in a parade of pride assembling.
Jewels are half buried underneath the ocean sand, strangled by gripping
tangling seaweed, choked.
A huge ship, which used to sail upon the sea, lies stranded with its
hull buried.
A dirty mast floateth aimlessly around the seabed like a lost feather
wandering.
A figurehead watcheth over all the precious belongings, like a guard
on watch.

*Charlotte Edmondson  (10)*
*St Mary's CE Primary School, Sale*


## HIDDEN TREASURES

A barrel like goblet there had lain.
In a galleon saileth strong like a powerful man.
Inside a rusty chest fantastic sparkling jewels.
Brass plated ship's wheel gracefully steers.
Gargantuan rum barrels deviously rolleth, like a round stone.
Bold figures proudly stand like a towering king.
Beautiful gold glints pricelessly.
The mast arrogantly stands like a chapel spire.

*Adam Martell  (10)*
*St Mary's CE Primary School, Sale*

## GOING SWIMMING

G  oing on a coach to the swimming bath.
O  blong float, swim with it if you can't swim.
I   ce-cold water.
N  ice water to swim in.
G  oggles go over your eyes, so you can see underwater.

S   wimming is great fun.
W  ater is so smooth.
I   n the water it is hot and out it is cold.
M  y favourite lesson is swimming.
M  rs Andrews is my swimming teacher.
I   love going to the swimming pool.
N  aughty people get sent out.
G  oing swimming makes me feel happy.

*Frankie Brown  (8)*
*St Vincent's RC Primary School, Knutsford*


## FOOTBALL

F   ootball rolls out on the pitch
O  wen comes out
O  ffside
T   ackling's great there
B   all goes right over
A  wesome goal
L   ook at that kick
L   iverpool win the cup.

*Cathal McGoohan  (8)*
*St Vincent's RC Primary School, Knutsford*

## BROTHER'S HABITS

Big, ugly, mean, kicking me all the time,
Rascal, sneaking into my room.
Outrageous, violent, selfish, giving me dead legs.
Telltale, always telling me off.
His deodorant stinks, taking my toys.
Everyday habits are awful, blackmailing me.
Rotten, taking the last biscuit.
Situation horrible, spooking me out.

Horrible, muttering, enemy.
Annoying, nasty, punching me.
Bigheaded bully, scaring me for no reason.
Idiot, screaming round the room.
Trying to be good, teacher's pet.
Sing a new song.

*Luke Fletcher (9)*
*St Vincent's RC Primary School, Knutsford*


## CHRISTMAS

C   is for crackers that bang
H   is for holly that is prickly
R   is for roast turkey which we eat
I    is for ivy that grows on the trees
S   is for snow which we play with
T   is for tree which we put decorations on
M   is for mince pies which we eat at Christmas
A   is for antlers which are on reindeer.
S   is for sledge on the snowy hills.

*Abigail Stones (8)*
*St Vincent's RC Primary School, Knutsford*

## ME AND CANDY
## CANDY MY CAT

When Candy learnt one
She walked on and on.
When Candy learnt two
She caught the flu.
When Candy learnt three
She learnt not to fight with me.
When Candy learnt four
She walked to the door.
When Candy learnt five
She went for a dive.
When Candy learnt six
She had a mix.
When Candy learnt seven
She knew about Heaven.
When Candy learnt eight
She found a mate.
When Candy learnt nine
She broke her spine.
When Candy learnt ten
She saw a lot of men.
When Candy learnt eleven
She went right up to Heaven.

Candy I miss you so much.

*Gemma Whyatt  (9)*
*St Vincent's RC Primary School, Knutsford*


## HAMSTER

I want a hamster,
Cute and cuddly.
I want a hamster,
A friend and all furry.

I want a hamster,
Running round his wheel.
I want a hamster
For a pet.

*Eleanor Regan  (10)*
*St Vincent's RC Primary School, Knutsford*

## THE ABOMINABLE SCIENCE TEST

Okay Cameron give out the books
Did I say throw?
No I didn't. I said give,
So why has Charles got a broken nose?

David, you can't have finished
Oh you've finished the date.
Well here's the sheet.
David you can't have finished,
In *five* seconds.

Well, then you can try this out while I check your book.
What do you mean the system won't load?
Okay who turned off the power?
Space invaders,
It should have been maths invaders.
Right then, let's do the answers to the test.
David, get off there,
No I will not let, Oh okay plug them in.
No I will not pay this two hundred pounds
To plug cables in and install some software.
Oh why did I start this lesson?

*David McCulloch  (10)*
*St Vincent's RC Primary School, Knutsford*

## WHY AM I SO STRANGE?

When I go to bed,
I hate being there.
When I wake up
I love being in bed.
Why am I so strange?
I believe in Harry Potter,
Though I know it's not true.
I think I'm someone else,
Though I know that's impossible.
Why am I so strange?
Why, why, why?

*Caitlin Julia Rowlands  (8)*
*St Vincent's RC Primary School, Knutsford*


## BIRTHDAYS

B    alloon popping.
I    t's so much fun.
R    edecorating the place
     it is hotter than the sun.
T    ara talking.
H    arry walking.
D    avid's legs tingling.
A    my singing
Y    oung children giggling.
S    weets shared out.

*Ishbel Johnson  (9)*
*St Vincent's RC Primary School, Knutsford*

## THE GORILLA LANDS

Rwanda the gorilla lands
where gorillas beat their chests with cupped hands.

Rwanda the gorilla lands
where gorillas roam in great big bands.

Rwanda the gorilla lands
where some gorillas don't have hands.

Rwanda the gorilla lands
where people kill gorillas for one hundred grand.

*George Morris  (8)*
*St Vincent's RC Primary School, Knutsford*


## CHRISTMAS

C   is for crackers that bang
H   is for hats in all different colours
R   is for roast which we like to eat
I    is for ivy that grows on the wall
S   is for snow which falls from the sky
T   is for tree with decorations
M   is for mince pies with icing on top
A   is for antlers stuck to a reindeer's head
S   is for sledge on snowy hills.

*Charlotte Perls  (8)*
*St Vincent's RC Primary School, Knutsford*

## THE MOUSE HOLE

Ah a mouse hole!
Under the stairs, there's a mouse hole.
In the night they creep out and
search for food.
In the morning they quickly rush
Back to the mouse hole.
Mum came down and blamed the dog.
The mice ate the food quietly
So no one knew they're there.
But still they come out in the night
and find food.

*Francesca Spada (8)*
*St Vincent's RC Primary School, Knutsford*



## NOW WHERE IS THAT DOG?

Now where is that dog?
I really cannot see.
I don't know where that dog is
Oh please, oh please, help me.
I can see his footprints
But I can't see the dog.
I wonder if that dog can
       hop, jump and jog.

*Jessica Whyatt (9)*
*St Vincent's RC Primary School, Knutsford*

## BIRTHDAYS

B  alloons bursting
I  nvitations received
R  elations rushing
T  ime ticking by
H  ats flying
D  isco music blaring
A  ll the wrapping
Y  o yo lights flashing
S  inging loudly.

*Amy Yardley (10)*
*St Vincent's RC Primary School, Knutsford*


## NUMERACY

N  egative numbers, numerator, number grids.
U  nderstanding units and tens.
M  ultiplying negative numbers.
E  stimating easy numbers.
R  egular shapes and sizes.
A  dding and subtracting numbers.
C  harts to show how much people like sweets.
Y  -axis shown on graphs.

*Amy Haughey (9)*
*St Vincent's RC Primary School, Knutsford*

## WALKING DOWN THE STREET ONE DAY

One day I was walking down the street,
And I saw a man with smelly feet.

They pinged and ponged,
And were awfully long.

That's the day I nearly died,
But my mum said it was one of my white lies.

The next day I went out with a peg up my nose,
I saw the same man with his mouth absolutely closed.

My mum called me in for tea,
And I saw a bumblebee.

I stood really still
Because I know it will.

Yes, sting me,
So I cried home, wee, wee, wee.

*Mica McDonald  (9)*
*St Vincent's RC Primary School, Knutsford*


## FAIRIES

Fairies wings flutter like magic
sparkling through the night sky.
Their eyes shine like little diamonds
when they say bye.
They leave trails of magic dust
going home hiding
under their pebble stones.

*Epiphany Harrop  (9)*
*St Vincent's RC Primary School, Knutsford*

## DREARY CLOUD

Every day, a dark dreary cloud,
Thunder's so, so very loud.
One day a dream of a light,
If the daytime could just be bright.
Would my dream all come true,
I want to see the sun brand new.
The trees struggle without both sides.
The sun and rain just do not collide.
People wonder of that day
When all will be revealed possibly in May.
The sky is just a big wonder.
People always make some blunders.
Answers have never come to this town
We never get our golden crown.

*Christopher Clarke (9)*
*St Vincent's RC Primary School, Knutsford*


## NUMERACY

N  eat work
U  se a ruler
M  ultiply, millimetre
E  qual estimating
R  ight angle
A  dding and average
C  entimetre
Y  ardstick.

*Francesca Whyatt (9)*
*St Vincent's RC Primary School, Knutsford*

## THE BLACKBOARD THAT WASN'T THERE

Ding dong! Ding dong! Went the doorbell,
A man came inside,
And stayed outside,
He said he had a blackboard
But Jim couldn't see it.

Jim drew on it
Even though he didn't,
He had a good look,
The writing had disappeared.

His mum came in,
Oh she did scream.
He had written on the wall again,
'I'm not speaking to you' she said,
Then spoke a little more.

Jim had a shock,
He fainted and woke up again.
When he got up he said something,
'I think I'm dead.'

*David McCabe  (10)*
*St Vincent's RC Primary School, Knutsford*


## ME AND MY FRIENDS

Me and my friends play out every day.
But in high school we are going to be friends forever.
When we leave high school, we are going to be popstars.
We are going to be singing friends forever
One for sorrow and making songs up.
      Me and my friends.

*Camilla Nixon  (9)*
*St Vincent's RC Primary School, Knutsford*

## GOING MAD

I'm going out to get some bread,
I hate those kids of mine.
You know I wish that I was dead,
Instead I'm getting my kids a shed.
One of them will lose their head,
But! The toilet seat, always up,
Door's always open.
I'm going mad and feeling sad,
Why am I alive?
There I was one day,
Standing by a beehive,
My job at school doesn't rule,
What is life without a wife?
But now I have to go,
Maybe tomorrow?

*Nathan Dodd  (10)*
*St Vincent's RC Primary School, Knutsford*


## WET PLAY

W  eary weather, wet play, we will have no fun today.
E  ating snacks in the classroom, teachers go into the staffroom.
T  easing children every day, what a rubbish play today.

P  laying football every day except for nasty wet plays.
L  earning every day so hard so why can't we get a good day.
A  ngry teacher stay away before she takes your play away.
Y  esterday we worked so hard, we deserve a sunny day.

*Marco Granata  (8)*
*St Vincent's RC Primary School, Knutsford*

## MY ROOM

'Thomas, go and tidy your room, it's a mess.'
'But Mum, I'm going out with my mates.'
'I don't care where you're going.'
Sometimes that boy can really get on my nerves.
'Come on Mum, I'll do it later.'
She's always going on at me to tidy my room.
'If you don't tidy your room I'll hang you up on the
washing line by your toenails!'
Do you see what I mean, he's a nuisance?
I don't care what she says.
I'm going out with my mates.
Just a bit of my amazing magic and I'll be outta here.
It's gone all quiet up there. I bet he's up to something.
He's plotting something. I can smell it.
Here she comes. Right on the count of three I run.
One, two three . . .
'I can hear you.
Where are you?
There you are.
I've known you for eleven years,
I know all of your tricks.'
'I'm going now. See ya!'
'Oh no you don't. You come back here right now!'

*Thomas Fletcher  (11)*
*St Vincent's RC Primary School, Knutsford*


## THE TEACHERS

Teachers are the best,
In the west.
They don't waste time,
They teach us rhythm and rhyme.
They got very cool cars
But they ain't got spars.

They stand so tall,
By the wall.
They stand so close
So we will do the most.
If teachers rule
Would we be cool?

*Emma Hobson  (11)*
*St Vincent's RC Primary School, Knutsford*


## WHAT'S LURKING IN THE BEDROOM?

What's lurking in the bedroom?
No one really knows.
People who go in there are driven to their doom,
Every day it's bigger, night by night it grows.

What's lurking in the bedroom?
You don't want to know.
There're ancient pairs of pants
And loads of rusty junk.

There's something living in there
Right between the junk.
Now I don't go in there,
So I don't get gobbled up!

I'm telling you this poem
From outside my house.
I should have been more careful
But know it's just all junk!

*Charles Miller  (10)*
*St Vincent's RC Primary School, Knutsford*

## The Nonsense Seasons

At the beginning of the end of the year,
The seasons will come out and appear,
First comes winter with its bright new flowers,
As they grow in the snow of the front garden.

Next comes autumn, with its sun so high.
Shining like a mirror reflecting its own beams into the sky.
Nobody has ever known why
It's like a tea tray  in the sky.

Third comes summer with its snow so white
Like the yolk of an egg which looks like a light.
Even though you wear shorts or T-shirts,
The snow bears down on the experts.

Last comes spring with its winds so cold,
But it's nothing like the things that I've just told.

*Cameron Mair  (10)*
*St Vincent's RC Primary School, Knutsford*

## Terrible

T   arantulas crawling
E   arwigs trawling
R   hinoceros goring
R   ats gnawing
I   nsects biting
B   rothers fighting
L   ions roaring
E   agles soaring.

*Amy Morgan  (8)*
*St Vincent's RC Primary School, Knutsford*

# THE VALENTINE'S DAY POEM

I like the way you walk.
The way you smile.
The way you talk.
You're really cool.
You're really fun.
In fact you're better than anyone.
I really, really like you,
You must know that for sure.
But I can't say any more.
So I'm writing to say
Happy Valentine's Day
With lots of hugs and kisses
And maybe one day I'll be your Mrs.

*Georgia Jackson  (11)*
*St Vincent's RC Primary School, Knutsford*

## SWIMMING

S   plashing about
W  et body
I    ce-cold water
M   outhful of water
M   rs Andrews teacher
I    ce-cold showers
N   ice dive ends with a splash
G   oggles covering eyes.

*Stephanie Trafford  (9)*
*St Vincent's RC Primary School, Knutsford*

## THE HUGE GIANTS

The huge giants is their name,
Playing football is their game.
They've never lost a single game,
Now they are in the hall of fame.

They're entering the Worthington Cup
With their captain Peter Sup
I hope they'll come home with their glory,
And an amazing story.

Maybe they'll win, maybe they won't
Never give up, don't, don't, don't.
If they lose they're still my favourite team
Shining like a golden beam.

*Rupert Heap  (9)*
*St Vincent's RC Primary School, Knutsford*

## SWEETS

Opal Fruits and Fruit Pastilles,
I have come to tell you that you are not
the only sweets in town.
There are Chewits, Jelly Babies and Milky Ways.
Opal Fruits I am sorry to tell you
that you have been invaded by Starbursts.

*Rosie Long  (9)*
*St Vincent's RC Primary School, Knutsford*

# MY PET GUINEA PIG

Guinness
A guinea pig
Waddles slowly around
Happy and always cuddly
My friend.

*Hannah Paver  (8)*
*St Vincent's RC Primary School, Knutsford*


# MY DAD . . .

My dad's face is round and chubby,
but his feet are rather grubby.

My dad's feet are very smelly,
especially when they have been in his welly.

My dad's eyes are nice and brown,
and his nose is red like a clown.

My dad has a very large belly,
it wobbles when he laughs whilst watching telly.

My dad likes eating Indian food,
especially when he's in the mood,
unfortunately this has repercussions and we have to hide
under the cushions.

*Emma Phillips  (9)*
*St Wilfrid's RC Primary School, Northwich*

# I Am A . . .

Sometimes I'm a swan
I peacefully glide
Beautiful and elegant
Along the riverside.

Sometimes I'm a deer
Silent and shy
When no one seems to notice me
So I try not to cry.

Sometimes I'm a spiteful fox
Swift and sly,
Silently I wait for my victim
Sneakily I lie.

Sometimes I'm a raging gorilla
And everyone is scared.
I'm angry and fierce
But I don't really care.

I have so many different moods
So I just can't see.
Which one I am, at least I'm sure,
I'm proud I'm me.

*Rebecca Cutbill  (10)*
*St Wilfrid's RC Primary School, Northwich*


# In The Middle Of The Park At Night

The park is quiet, the park is still,
You can see moonlight above the hill.
The swings are swinging
Gently the rain drops on the slide.
The roundabout going round in the middle of the night.

Fallen, broken, branches, leaves scattered around.
Trees shivering, rabbits on the ground.
Grass swaying, seesaw still.
I can still see the moonlight above the hill.

*Kate Frazer  (9)*
*St Wilfrid's RC Primary School, Northwich*


## MOOD POEM

Sometimes I'm an owl,
Silently, sweeping,
Gracefully, gliding,
Watching, waiting,
Swooping, hooting,
Catching, tearing,
Satisfied.

Sometimes I'm a lion,
Roaring, snarling,
Paving, padding,
Running, leaping,
Smelling, prodding,
Scratching, snatching,
Back into the forest.

Sometimes I'm a rabbit,
Hip hop,
Jump, bump,
Funny, friendly,
Happy, hoppy,
Leap, run.
Then away.

*Anna Cartwright  (10)*
*St Wilfrid's RC Primary School, Northwich*

## SNAKE

He
    Slithers, sneakily
   through the treacherous
     forest, animals
       fleeing from
         his deathly detergent.
           Viper venomous
             teeth shining
               in the sun
             while slashing
           through tight
        spaces. Twist
     and turning
   while hissing
     like the howling
       wind, living in
         the dangerous
           Forest, savagely
             lurking in
             an abandoned
               Ship!

*James Turrell  (9)*
*St Wilfrid's RC Primary School, Northwich*


## GLASSES

Just because I wear glasses
People pick on me.
They call me names like four eyes
And say I'm as blind as can be.

People try and trip me up
They stick their foot out at me.
Sometimes I fall over
And hurt my hands and knees.

Just because I wear glasses
No one's my friend.
No one ever plays with me
It's just never ever fair.

*Jemima Hollingworth  (8)*
*St Wilfrid's RC Primary School, Northwich*


## NIGHT

Night is waiting, waiting for the sun to go down
behind the orange hill.
Rising from her raincloud, she calls her mare,
steps on and glides off into the darkness.

She wears a cloak of finest silk.
Below her waist a blue whale's skin.
And above her ear you may see,
a rose half-covered by her star filled hair.

Her face is thoughtful, full of worries.
Balls of fire and ice, her eyes.
A golden smile upon her face
Her hair is black and full of silver stars.

Upon her nightmare she soars across the skies,
spreading her peppermint and lavender smell
she spreads out dreams.
And coughs out nightmares.

Night is waiting, waiting for the sun to come up from
behind the orange hill.
Sinking into her raincloud,
she steps off her mare and glides off into the darkness.

*Emma Draffin  (11)*
*St Wilfrid's RC Primary School, Northwich*

## I REMEMBER

Tasting the smooth soft mousse in my red-hot mouth,
Tasting the wobbly jelly inside my warm mouth,
Tasting the cold fresh apple of the tree,
Tasting the hot scalding chips,
Tasting the spicy curry sauce for tea.

Smelling the pollen in the sweet juicy flower,
Smelling the salty seawater with my cold nose,
Smelling the sweet watermelon in the fridge,
Smelling the chocolate in maths,
Smelling the fresh air first thing in the morning.

Looking at the strange object in my hand,
Looking at the moon in the dark night sky.
Looking at everyone while I come in,
Looking at the sun up above,
Looking at the people down the narrow street.

Listening to the noise in the classroom next door,
Listening to the birds sing,
Listening to the crying from the house next door,
Listening to the last words as I leave the door,
Listening to my brother row with my sister.

Touching the cold pen I write with,
Touching the cat that purrs around me.
Touching the soft comforting pillow on which I lie,
Touching the teddy asleep in my bed,
Touching my book to close for bed.

*Jennifer Schofield (10)*
*St Wilfrid's RC Primary School, Northwich*

## NIGHT

I met at eve, the queen of night
Kind and caring
Offering sweet dreams
As she casts her shadow afar.

Her pearls were stars
And the moon her lantern
She shone her light
Which danced among the clouds.

But a dark side she does have!
As she crept through the town
Like the panther cat
Bringing dreams of fear and fright
Throughout the town, throughout the night.

Her dark hair was enlaced with stars
Her garb was a deep shade of burgundy
Her crown that rested on her brow
Was made of pearls which shone so bright.

As dawn creeps in
Her enemy approaches
She sets off for her flight
And click, click she's gone.

I met at eve, the queen of night
Kind and caring
Offering sweet dreams
As she casts her shadow afar.

*Rebecca Boyle  (10)*
*St Wilfrid's RC Primary School, Northwich*

## WHY ARE BIG SISTERS SO GOOD?

We guard our little sisters
Even when they are naughty and silly.
We love them very much
Even when they are a pain, shouting and screaming,
Not helping or following the rules.

Sometimes little sisters can be nice
That's when it can be fun to be a big sister.
We can cuddle and giggle and hold hands together,
We can play and be friends.

Big sisters are great, they love and care
They are kind and sharing and put up with a lot.
I know why big sisters are good,
That's because I am one!

*Genevieve Reynolds  (8)*
*St Wilfrid's RC Primary School, Northwich*


## HORSES

Every Saturday
Whatever the weather
I put on my hat and my coat and my boots.

And go with Mummy to ride on a horse
Over the fields, and the lanes and the heather.

But we're not very good at riding yet,
So we ride in a circle in the barn.
Oh well!

*Felicity Lewis  (9)*
*St Wilfrid's RC Primary School, Northwich*

## PLAYING TIGER

I have a tiger in me.

Quietly walking towards his prey
*Pounce* ripping and tearing it
With his sharp claws.
Waiting for silence as it speeds
Back to his den.
Sniffing out trespassers on his way.
Quietly he sneaks back into the den
and settles down for a quiet night.

> But now that I think
> Maybe I don't like tigers.

*Brian Byrne  (10)*
*St Wilfrid's RC Primary School, Northwich*


## THE HAPPY LITTLE SNOWMAN

A rotund snowman
Icy cold
Best friends with Jack Frost you know
His coal black eyes
Glisten in the moonlight
His 24 carat gold nose
Is one any snowman would envy
A fat, happy little snowman
Everything about him gleams
A fat, happy little snowman.
> Fast asleep.

*Isabel Murray  (9)*
*St Wilfrid's RC Primary School, Northwich*

## DARKNESS

Something lurks in the air
It only comes out at night
It's always there
It can give us a fright.

What's that over there?
It's crawling in the night
It's hiding in the air
Waiting to take our sight.

It will crawl up your spine,
To meet you.
It's shadowy hand will greet you.

It can scare us
It feels like killing
It will really tear us
When it's willing.

The cunning, slithering darkness!

*Emma Hitch  (10)*
*St Wilfrid's RC Primary School, Northwich*



## LIFE WITHOUT CARS

It's like having a bike with no wheels
You would have to walk to get your meals
There wouldn't be much noise
And boys wouldn't have many toys.

There wouldn't be fun car races
Or films with high speed chases
Lots of people would have no work
But our world would be lovely and green.

No long queues to park the car
Finding the right money
No petrol stations
That would be funny.

*Michael Thomas  (8)*
*St Wilfrid's RC Primary School, Northwich*


## THE T-REX IN THE CITY

One day I met a T-rex
And he had big black eyes,
His skin was green and scaly,
His huge teeth were a surprise!

One day I met a T-rex
Stomping down my street,
Squashing homes and smashing cars,
With his huge and stinky feet!

It came across a river
Looked at it and said
I am a scary T-rex
But I can't swim -
So I'll catch the bus instead!

One day I met a T-rex,
Jumping on my house,
Up he went, down it went,
Down with all my bros'!

*David Rattigan  (9)*
*St Wilfrid's RC Primary School, Northwich*

## MY MARSHMALLOW FRIEND

Silvery slime,
Makes me shiver,
Over the rain covered leaves.
The trail led me, but I stopped at the river.
Stop! Wait! I saw something slither.
I see a funny looking stone.
But no! It's a tiny mobile phone.
With two tiny little mobile phones.
Slowly I approach,
With a frown,
I see it's a snail (called Slowly),
Wearing a golden crown,
To match his silvery trail.
Silently, it slithers away,
But I'll see my marshmallow friend,
Another day.

*Amy Fallon (10)*
*St Wilfrid's RC Primary School, Northwich*


## MY PET

My pet is green,
He's never mean.
My pet is kind,
I don't know why adults mind.
My pet is a dragon
I call him Jim.
All the kids love him
And he loves them.
But he can only eat one or two!
Well, maybe a few!

*Leah Whyment (8)*
*St Wilfrid's RC Primary School, Northwich*

## THE SNAKE

Silently
slithering
through the
hissing wind
on the hot
scorching
desert.
His sharp
pointed tail
whipping the
warm sand.
Eyes red
as the fires flame,
blazing as he
searches the dusty desert
for his prey.

*Jane Edwards  (9)*
*St Wilfrid's RC Primary School, Northwich*


## MY DOGISH POEM

I have a dog in me
Barking, making my tummy growl.
Chasing cats up a tree.
It tears and rips
Trying to tear away its lead,
Waiting for its master to
            Return.

*Michael Jones  (9)*
*St Wilfrid's RC Primary School, Northwich*

## THE ANIMALS INSIDE

I am a deer
Beautiful and calm
Hiding shyly
In the green.
I am a dog
Bouncy and fun,
Sometimes lazy,
Lying in the sun.
I am a spider
Crawling and scuttling,
Still as a statue,
Waiting to pounce,
I am a swan,
Gliding gracefully,
Through the water,
Calm and peaceful,
The animals inside.

*Colleen O'Sullivan (9)*
*St Wilfrid's RC Primary School, Northwich*


## CHATTY ME

I have a parrot in me,
Annoyingly fluttering around,
Painfully pecking,
Cheekily talking back when you least expect it,
Swinging, smashing scaringly,
Saying words which have already been said,
Flying like fighter planes at ten miles an hour,
Endlessly chattering pointless words,
That's me!

*Dean McGuinness (9)*
*St Wilfrid's RC Primary School, Northwich*

## A LIGHT BULB

Hanging waiting
for the fingers of
power to shoot
through its veiny wires,
to make it as bright as the sun.
Its fat rotund body
isn't very heavy,
actually it's really light.
Whenever its body gets into action
it kills; hammers;
murders the darkness.
Then it suddenly becomes
powerless!

*Richard Tranter  (10)*
*St Wilfrid's RC Primary School, Northwich*


## THE DUCKLING

Scared to be fed by hand
Cute and cuddly,
If you try to pick me up
I will swim gracefully off.
Yet, if you're still and gentle you might manage
Just to get me to sit on your hand,
Then you'll get to stroke me gently
If you should startle me
I will run or swim away.
But I am friendly to the bone,
I will not hurt you.
Yet, if I do it would be more like a tickle for I'm not strong.

*Michelle Huggon  (9)*
*St Wilfrid's RC Primary School, Northwich*

## INSIDE MY HEAD

There's a deep dark cave
Inside my head.
Where you hear spooky sounds.
An owl cries like a ghost
And a snake slithers through dried up leaves.

There's a deep dark cave
Inside my head,
Where you see shadows dance,
Fireflies flicker or glow
And a night-light comes closer and closer towards you.

There's a deep dark cave
Inside my head,
Where you hear a mother bear and her cubs growl in the night.
Where you come in and never come out.

There's a deep dark cave
Inside my head,
Where there are freaky thoughts that give you goosebumps
And dreams turn into nightmares.

*Avril Wood  (9)*
*St Wilfrid's RC Primary School, Northwich*


## I Am A . . .

Sometimes I am a dog
All playful and jumpy
I never want to stop playing
If you don't play with me, I will get grumpy.

Sometimes I am a deer
Silent, still and shy.
I don't dare come out
I try not to cry.

Sometimes I am a dolphin
Very playful and friendly.
I like to make new friends
Even though I have lots already.

*Alex Plant  (9)*
*St Wilfrid's RC Primary School, Northwich*


## MOOD POEM

I have a gorilla in me,
Fiercely fighting, physically banging and jumping.
Raging and rampaging.
Snapping and pouncing with anger.
Climbing trees and snapping branches.

I have an elephant in me.
Stomping sternly through the open forest,
Fiercely shaking my trunk,
Regretfully knocking down trees and rocks.

Sometimes I feel like a snake,
Slithering sneakily through the green grass,
Dodging treacherous quicksand in a zigzag path.
Then pouncing on my prey with a squeeze
That's me.

*Ben Millar  (10)*
*St Wilfrid's RC Primary School, Northwich*

## MY PERSONALITY

I have a cat in me,
It scrabbles and scrambles.
It's sometimes sad,
It hates water,
Then it is mischievous.

I have a cat in me,
It's playful and pounces.
It leaps and springs,
Ever restless.

I love this cat in me,
It's my best friend,
Nobody will ever take it away from me,
It's my personality.

*Shanice Ashley (9)*
*St Wilfrid's RC Primary School, Northwich*


## MY SISTER DOMINIQUE

People think she's lovely
People think she's sweet
But she calls me names
Names, I can't repeat.

She gets all the attention
She pretends she cares.
But she's really nasty
When she pulls and tugs my hair.

*Geneviève Darwin (8)*
*St Wilfrid's RC Primary School, Northwich*

## THE MOODS I FEEL

Sometimes I feel like a swan shimmering on the glassy water,
gliding silently through the night.
Sometimes I feel like an owl swooping through the air,
Lonely waiting for its prey.
Sometimes I feel like a deer hiding shyly in the grass.
Sometimes I feel like a mouse so small and unnoticed,
Sometimes I feel like an elephant stamping through the jungle,
Sometimes I feel like a lion, ready to pounce raging with anger.
Sometimes I feel like a whale swishing through the water.
That's me.

*Claire Campbell (9)*
*St Wilfrid's RC Primary School, Northwich*


## SOMETIMES I FEEL LIKE

Some days I am like a dolphin splashing about
I am like a dolphin needing lots of attention
I am like a dolphin always eating.

Sometimes like a cat jumping about
I am like a cat playing about
I am like a cat being friendly.

I feel like a swan gliding in the water
I am like a swan secretly sleeping
I am like a swan my wing is my charm.

*Catherine Lewis (9)*
*St Wilfrid's RC Primary School, Northwich*

## I HAVE A LION IN ME

I have a lion in me,
King of the jungle.
Sprinting and springing,
Creeping and pouncing,
Roaring and growling,
Biting and scratching,
Ripping at his prey,
Sipping at the great lake.
I have a lion in me.

*Cameron Mackay (9)*
*St Wilfrid's RC Primary School, Northwich*


## DIFFERENT MOODS

I'm sometimes a crocodile with a smirking grin.
Or sometimes a swan gently floating across the lake.
Or a golden eagle soaring through the sky
faster than light.
Sometimes I'm a gorilla pouncing and bouncing all around.
Or sometimes an owl lonely all alone.
That is me.

*John Peyton (10)*
*St Wilfrid's RC Primary School, Northwich*

## MY MOOD POEM

I have a gorilla in me,
Snarling with rage.
Pounding fists on my chest,
Grouchy, mean, stubborn,
frowning, fierce, stressed,
Stamping, stomping,
I have a gorilla in me today.

*Christopher Timm (9)*
*St Wilfrid's RC Primary School, Northwich*

## DARK EMOTION

It tunnels,
Deep within your eternal heart and soul,
It seeks out the love you so dearly cherish,
It is worse than the cruel emotion of sadness,
Worse than the feeling of pain and anguish,
It is hatred,
The Devil's emotion,
Cast down upon us at the dawn of time,
To thwart our happiness.

*Richard Roper (11)*
*Sandiway County Primary School*

## TRIUMPH

Rising from the meadows confronting his destiny he walks,
people gather from his kin
they wake spurring him on
as his destiny becomes closer,
the dragon's lair, the cave draws,
the daunting picture coming out of the gloom,
opening its dark passage,
awaiting its triumph or death,
the omen grows nearer.

In he goes, no one shall follow,
into the dark mountain,
fear crawling like spiders up his nimble body.
The courage fighting them off,
he comes to an emotional standstill,
but still he walks,
his destiny growing ever closer and ever closer still.
He trembles in its wake,
preparing his destiny,
his sword and dagger at hilt pleading to get out,
pleading to show justice.

He slips forward against the wall
sweat from fear and heat pulling the blade from its hilt,
preparing for his destiny.
His heart racing,
he runs waking the slumber and thrashing his blade on the hide,
but nigh it only made scratch.
Its wing beats throw him back,
he looks around the slumber chamber hoping for bow and quill,
to bleed the under belly,
but none is found.
He dashes for the silver shield,
running for refuge from the raging fire of the breath.

He dives under his saviour,
denying death's hope,
he waits whilst fire rushes past,
to predict his next move.

When the rage stopped he jumped under the belly
and plunged into its icy blood
pulling the sword, clear from the gash,
he rolled and ran up the passage again,
his heart racing as the daunting shadow of his opponent dims,
he has won his destiny.
The light, the brilliant light of day,
shone into his bloodshot eyes,
no more than that.
He walks back across the meadows,
more gather round and rejoice in his triumph.

*James Pearson  (11)*
*Sandiway County Primary School*


## THE HERO'S FUNERAL

Silence has fallen
Forceful emotions carried,
The loss of a friend.

Life has carried on,
Never such a vast killing,
Since the First World War.

Life has carried on,
The vast killings have triggered
The Second World War.

*Douglas Pinnington  (10)*
*Sandiway County Primary School*

# THE INVISIBLE DEATH

The scythe brung down upon his fears,
Binding thunder clear, to clash to tears.
The power taunts the breathing rage,
And blood pulls through and across the page.
But soon his tale of breath did touch the soil,
For underneath his skin was a thought of toil.

His spoke crusted in vein to live again,
Fast death came swift to trap in the pen.
The red blood was cooked to have taste once more,
But once more was not as it spilt for pain.
The mind cold could not bear his twisted coil,
As near it snapped to burn and boil.

Through searching fog to block the light,
He sought the sword of heaving might.
Its heart did crawl when torn to splits,
Banished to hell into the cremating pits to blitz.
None did see the fate that bound him loyal,
As earth is special and none shall spoil.

*Alexander Crompton (10)*
*Sandiway County Primary School*


## POLLUTION

The small creature rooted for food.
Pushing aside leaves from the trees.
Its home was found.
Cities were built.
Creatures died, creatures became extinct.
Pollution came, we ruined our world.
Soon there may be no creatures, no life!

*Emma Molyneux (10)*
*Sandiway County Primary School*

# HIDDEN TREASURES

Bubbling away,
lost forever,
that precious ring
dropped forever.

The vast land,
shocked by the misleadings,
the volcano had struck
dead millions.

But the ring,
that precious ring
dropped, never returned.

The old owner,
nothing left,
hidden never found.

Crying tears,
the object gone,
never to be uncovered.

That ring!
That ring!
gone, gone,
took away,
finished,
ended,
gone.

*Josie Capel  (10)*
*Sandiway County Primary School*

## SADNESS

I once had it,
It was taken from me,
I want it back, I'm desperate for it,
People's mourning for me is piecemeal,
Praying for me is fraudulent,
It wasn't pestilence that made me go away,
It was the lonely feeling of sadness that formed my final day.
I was paltry to everyone.
The flower fields I walk in are odourless
Life was always a blur, an obscure mist
of anguish and desperation.
I'm left as an oddment, a melancholy memory . . .

*James Hocking  (10)*
*Sandiway County Primary School*


## WAR PLANET

War planet red, red like anger, anger like Ares.
We've never been there, but we know so much about it.
The towering volcanoes,
Spewing life-taking lava,
The aroma of death.
Nothing can survive.

Red dust the essence of life that used to be.
Craters, birthmarks of the landscape.
The distance from the giant freezes the caps.
War planet moves into an eternal ice age.

*Mhairi Macritchie  (10)*
*Sandiway County Primary School*

## FUTURE LIVES

You come, you go,
You travel, you return,
You pick up an image, inspired,
You put it to the test, hopeful,
Patience it takes, patience it drains,
Energy it requires, energy you lose,
Knowledge compulsory, knowledge, is sapped,
Conclusions destroyed, conclusions revealed,
Desire or despair,
The final achievement awaits . . .
Congratulations . . .
Or commiseration?

*William Eggleston  (10)*
*Sandiway County Primary School*


## ICY TREASURE

It sits there, frozen,
Children play in snow and ice,
It comes within the snow.

The creature weakens,
The months go by and heat comes,
The creature's dying.

Summer comes quickly,
The creature dies out, slowly
Will he be back? . . .

*Alex Frommert  (10)*
*Sandiway County Primary School*

## The Night's Sun

He sits among his winking eyes,
Shining on the darkened canvas.
He lives among the falling rocks
not feeling any of their hits.

He circles his captor of his soul,
not caring about his disappearing life.
He is flung by his mighty father
but has no mother to call for.

He hooks his prey and pulls it in,
but makes the horses stir.
He shows people the way when they are lost,
but they do not thank him for his kindness.

*Tom Whitehead  (11)*
*Sandiway County Primary School*


## Mysteries

The enigma,
Is erased,
Many tragedies happened.

Joy and prosperity may be there,
Voyages to unfamiliar worlds,
Savage wars, fought by tribes.

God's dark secrets
One different world from ours.
Nothing is known of this world,
Empty space in time.

*Tom Phillips  (10)*
*Sandiway County Primary School*

## ENCOUNTERING DARKNESS

Immoral darkness, quivering true,
Shifty eyes, reaching for you.
Death's departure, infinite preparation,
Night-time lurches, light desperation.
Luminescence ascends, the morbid has gone,
The victor, the light, the one.

*Joanna Laurence  (10)*
*Sandiway County Primary School*


## THE FUTURE IS A MYSTERY

F   orget our world, get on to somewhere else.
U   nder, beneath the hidden secrets
T   he different ways to help us,
U   nravel the air, sky and earth
R   unning out will never happen
E   verybody amazed it's the . . . Future.

*Amy Johnson  (10)*
*Sandiway County Primary School*


## BIG AND BLUE

As I come off the soft, smooth sand,
The wavy whales-way sprays cold salty water,
Fighting against the oars of my boat,
The whales-way splashes and crashes against the boat and me.

*Victoria Monk  (10)*
*Sandiway County Primary School*

## WHY?

Some people in space
Some people on the ground
Some people wonder why
Some people just know how.

Some people can't be bothered
Some people have an urge
Some people stand and stare
Some people change the world.

*Katie Dunn  (10)*
*Sandiway County Primary School*


## IN THE MAGIC ROOM

In the magic room I saw . . .
Jars of stars
Loads of toads,
What on earth could they be for?

In the magic room I saw . . .
Mugs of bugs,
Pockets of lockets,
What on earth could they be for?

In the magic room I saw . . .
Pools of tools,
Blocks of socks
What on earth could they be for?

They work magic for me!

*Stefan Szymkowiak  (8)*
*Wellfield Junior School*

# THE MAGIC ROOM

Inside the magic room I saw . . .
Pools of fools,
Plates of mates,
What on earth are they for?

Inside the magic room I saw . . .
Bags of hags,
Sets of nets,
What on earth are they for?

Inside the magic room I saw . . .
Vats of rats,
Ladles of cradles,
What on earth are they for?

Inside the magic room I saw . . .
Bowls of shoals,
Dishes of fishes,
What on earth are they for?

Inside the magic room I saw . . .
Pairs of stairs,
Pots of dots,
What on earth are they for?

*David Laybourn (9)*
*Wellfield Junior School*

## SMOKING

Smoking, smoking,
Causes choking,
So listen carefully
If you think I'm joking.

It fills your lungs
With black gooey tar,
And if you smoke,
You won't get very far.

There really is only you to blame,
When you light up that little flame,
If you just stop to weigh up the cost,
You'll start to wonder who is the boss?

No one will come near you,
If you smoke, so don't think
This is a joke.
With dirty teeth and smelly breath,
That last cigarette will be your *death.*

*Andrew Davin  (9)*
*Wellfield Junior School*


## BABIES

Babies kick and babies crawl,
That's what babies do.
Oh babies,
They're awful.

Slide their potties down the hall,
That's what babies do,
Oh babies,
They're terrible.

Babies cry and babies yell,
That's what babies do.
Oh babies,
They're awful.

This one has a funny smell,
That's what babies do,
Oh babies,
They're terrible.

*Amy McAdam (9)*
*Wellfield Junior School*


## FRIGHT OR THE COLD?

He noticed the sun disappear behind a mountain,
Blackness spreading over the endless sky,
Suddenly there was a sensation
Running through his body,
Was it fright or just the cold?

A  badger hurried blindly across his path,
An owl hooted and stared
With its bright eyes glistening,
He started to run.
He ran and ran and ran . . .

Lightning struck a nearby tree,
The rain pounded on his face,
He could bear it no longer
He let out an awful bloodcurdling shriek,
He was lost . . .

*Katherine Gore (9)*
*Wellfield Junior School*

## THE MAGIC ROOM

Inside the magic room I saw
Pockets of lockets, dishes of wishes,
What on earth could they be for?

Inside the magic room I saw
Jars of bars, chests of vests,
What on earth could they be for?

Inside the magic room I saw
Pools of tools, bins of tins,
What on earth could they be for?

Inside the magic room I saw
Boxes of socks, loads of toads,
What on earth could they be for?

Inside the magic room I saw
Mugs of bugs, packets of jackets,
What on earth could they be for?

*Emma Challinor  (9)*
*Wellfield Junior School*


## PETS GALORE!

I have two dogs, two very cute dogs,
And those two dogs are called Pog and Zog.
And those two dogs have a chewy toy
One dog's a girl and one's a boy.

I have three cats, three very cute cats,
And those three cats sit on their mats.
And those little mats are a purple-pink pattern,
And the mats are made out of rattan.

I have four lizards, four very cute lizards.
They can't sit out in very cold blizzards.
The lizards are green and red,
Sometimes they scuttle in my bed.

I have five mice, five very cute mice,
Their personality is very nice.
They like to eat green mouldy cheese,
And wobble about on their knees!

*Katie Marshall (9)*
*Wellfield Junior School*


## PARENTS

Parents moan
Parents scream
Some parents are very mean.

'Tidy your room'
'Wash the pots,
You're no longer in your baby cots.'

'Do this,
Do that,
Don't forget to feed the cat!'

All they do is
*Shout! Shout! Shout!*
I feel like pulling a piggie's snout.

But I suppose they're not all that bad,
If you think extra hard,
Without our parents we'd all be mards!

*Becky McGeorge (9)*
*Wellfield Junior School*

## GALAXIES

Galaxy, galaxy oh where are you?
Galaxy, galaxy, what to do.
Galaxy, galaxy, high in the sky,
Galaxy, galaxy, why are you so high?
Galaxy, galaxy, so dark and so bright
Galaxy, galaxy oh which should I write?
Galaxy, galaxy so far away,
Galaxy, galaxy will I see one another day?
Galaxy, galaxy in the Milky Way,
Galaxy, galaxy I will watch your big sway.
Galaxy, galaxy I know you're there,
Galaxy, galaxy in no thin air.
Galaxy, galaxy all different shapes,
Galaxy, galaxy made from different dates.
Galaxy, galaxy I'll see you one day,
Galaxy, galaxy, just a different day.

*Ashley Drinkwater (8)*
*Wellfield Junior School*


## BONFIRE NIGHT

On Bonfire Night a rocket goes off
As I eat the treacle toffee from my pocket.
As I drink my Coke.
My ears are starting to hurt from the sound
As I hear the cat pound down from the fence.
As it is nearly time to go I bang my toe on a stone.
I quickly run to answer the phone.

*Danielle O'Brien (10)*
*Woodheys Primary School*

## WE HAD A LITTLE BONFIRE NIGHT!

We had a little Bonfire Night
Once it said in the newspaper
that Diwali has to end at night.
Oh what a disaster,
But still it's fine.
In India there is a festival
It's my favourite,
It's a bit like Bonfire Night,
But it has fireworks and shooting rockets
like the beam of light.

*Yashika Walia (10)*
*Woodheys Primary School*


## BONFIRE NIGHT

The crackle, the bang,
The flash of purple, pink, blue and red.
*Crackle, sizzle* goes the bonfire,
As sparks fly in the air and
*Snap!* goes the fire.
While more wood goes on in pairs
Higher and higher goes the fireworks then
*Bang* and a colour of cloud forms in the pitch-black sky.

*Christopher Lunt (9)*
*Woodheys Primary School*

## TURNABOUT POEM - SCHOOL

The gush of children oozed
into the dormant classroom.
'Sit down' said the teacher with
sparks erupting from his ears.
The children sat down,
this was the teacher that everyone fears.
Still red hot and crackling he exploded.
Out of his ears molten lava flowed.
The room set ablaze and the classroom was
no longer dormant.
It was one boiling red-hot ash.
Burning books spat out of the windows.
Pencils, rubbers and rulers.

*Jonathan Stead  (10)*
*Woodheys Primary School*


## WHEN A WITCH'S SPELL IS CAST

When a witch's spell is cast
you must never go past.
There it lies in the cauldron
it must always be revolting.

When the witch's cat
gets very, very fat,
the witch can never turn
into a bat.

*Laura Colwell  (10)*
*Woodheys Primary School*

## HALLOWE'EN

The people from the dead
Are coming back tonight
Making people scared
And giving kids a fright.

It's time for bats and rats
And even spooky cats
Kids go out to play
Because it's a special day.

Pumpkins are on the floor
Ghouls are knocking at the door.
It is time to go to our beds
And rest our sleepy heads.

*Kate Green  (9)*
*Woodheys Primary School*

## TANGO

Tango is my fat cat,
At night she chases bats, rats and other cats.
When she comes in she does her funny act,
She sits in her tatty hat
And waits for her owner Pat to give her,
Her tatty play rat and purrs on Pat's knee,
Very happy she seems to be.

*Kesiah Pickford  (9)*
*Woodheys Primary School*

## WHY ME?

Why can't I bound up the stairs?
Why can't I leap into a squashy armchair?
Why can't I stamp my feet when I'm very mad?
Why can't I jump into my mum's arms when I'm sad?
Why can't I run, skip and hop?
Why can't I circle the floor with my mum's giant mop?
Why can't I swoop down the slide in the park?
Why can't I sneak downstairs and have a feast in the dark?

But I can play basketball in a wheelchair.
I can swim just by using my arms.
I can race in my wheelchair.
I can be lazy and not fetch my mum's glasses.
I can still play table tennis.
And I can still have fun with my friends.

*Jessica Overton  (9)*
*Woodheys Primary School*

## SNAIL

Snails are round, slimy and slow.
He likes things that glow.
He has a curly shell.
His slime is like gel.
He has no legs.
His eyes are like pegs.

*Bethan Lawrence  (10)*
*Woodheys Primary School*

## SCHOOL

Teachers raging with boiling spit,
Children waiting for keep fit.
Teachers going completely wild,
Temperature boiling for every child.

The headmistress is in for a shock
The classrooms now are crumbly rock.
People gushing to and fro,
Children running high and low.

The noise is spitting, boiling, raging.
Teachers mad, children gazing!
Lunchtime is coming very near,
Waiting for the bell though, they can't hear!

***Charlotte Simpson***
***Woodheys Primary School***


## PUMPKINS WITH CANDLES IN

Pumpkins with candles in,
Candy wrappers in the bin,
Trick or treating round the street,
Costumes and masks sewn in neat,
Telling ghost stories in torchlight,
Having nightmares in the night.

***Rachel Colwell  (10)***
***Woodheys Primary School***

## WHY ME!

Why me?
Why me stuck in a wheelchair?
To know I won't be the next David Beckham,
Oh why me not being able to dance?
Why me not being able to take my dog for a walk?
Why me, not able to play hockey?
I can't beat my brother up when he's bullying me.
Oh it sucks being stuck in this chair.

But who cares,
I can do other things,
I can still beat most people in a wheelchair race,
I can swim faster than my weedy little friends.
My arm muscles are massive.
So who cares.
And now I don't have to do chores.
I'll still be able to play with my friends,
And that's what counts,
And I'm still alive.

*Ryan Sweetman  (9)*
*Woodheys Primary School*


## BIG BALLOON

Floating away in the middle of the day,
Floating high in the sky,
There's no sound,
Bobbing around,
Big balloon made friends with a racoon.

*Ellie Gowland  (9)*
*Woodheys Primary School*

## THE SCHOOL

The teacher is a dormant volcano ready to explode any minute.
The children run riot around the classroom wildly
hot volcanoes already exploding.
The teacher's face is a fiery red.
The children scream and shout as they dash through the door
gushing into the playground like molten lava.
The teacher is mad, the teacher is frighteningly fierce.
*Boom! Crackle! Boil!* she is dangerously deafeningly loud,
and no longer dormant, she is an active volcano.
She has exploded!

*Elizabeth Dunn (11)*
*Woodheys Primary School*

## I WISH . . .

I wish that chocolate grew on trees
Or sweeties grew on walls,
That Mars bars grew on blades of grass,
Or Twixs came the size of balls.

Fat ones, slim ones, striped ones too.
Big fat sticky ones that always stick.
Small tiny ones as small as an ant,
Strong minty ones are easy to lick.

*Emma Clowes (10)*
*Woodheys Primary School*

## SCHOOL

The crackling teacher was pumping toxic clouds
And the children were suffocating constantly.
The bell ring deafening and the children flowed through the school
like bubbling molten lava.

At the end of the day the teachers are dormant and they turn into steam.
They burn out and become extinct,
And stop being mean.

*Michael Roberts  (11)*
*Woodheys Primary School*


## SNAILS

Snails are round, slimy and slow.
He likes things that glow.
He has a curly shell,
His slime is like gel.
He has no legs,
His eyes are like pegs.

*Aishah Essaih*
*Woodheys Primary School*